LITERATURE FROM CRESCENT MOON PUBLISHING

Sexing Hardy: Thomas Hardy and Feminism
by Margaret Elvy

Thomas Hardy's Jude the Obscure: A Critical Study
by Margaret Elvy

Thomas Hardy's Tess of the d'Urbervilles: A Critical Study
by Margaret Elvy

Stepping Forward: Essays, Lectures and Interviews
by Wolfgang Iser

Andrea Dworkin
by Jeremy Mark Robinson

German Romantic Poetry: Goethe, Novalis, Heine, Hölderlin
by Carol Appleby

D.H. Lawrence: Infinite Sensual Violence
by M.K. Pace

D.H. Lawrence: Symbolic Landscapes
by Jane Foster

Samuel Beckett Goes Into the Silence
by Jeremy Mark Robinson

*In the Dim Void: Samuel Beckett's Late Trilogy:
Company, Ill Seen, Ill Said and Worstward Ho*
by Gregory Johns

Amorous Life: John Cowper Powys and the Manifestation of Affectivity
by H.W. Fawkner

Postmodern Powys: New Essays on John Cowper Powys
by Joe Boulter

Rethinking Powys: Critical Essays on John Cowper Powys
edited by Jeremy Mark Robinson

Thomas Hardy and John Cowper Powys: Wessex Revisited
by Jeremy Mark Robinson

Julia Kristeva: Art, Love, Melancholy, Philosophy, Semiotics
by Kelly Ives

Luce Irigaray: Lips, Kissing, and the Politics of Sexual Difference
by Kelly Ives

Helene Cixous I Love You: The Jouissance of Writing
by Kelly Ives

Emily Dickinson: *Selected Poems*
selected and introduced by Miriam Chalk

Petrarch, Dante and the Troubadours: The Religion of Love and Poetry
by Cassidy Hughes

Dante: *Selections From the Vita Nuova*
translated by Thomas Okey

Friedrich Hölderlin: *Selected Poems*
translated by Michael Hamburger

Walking In Cornwall
by Ursula Le Guin

André Gide
Fiction and Fervour

André Gide
Fiction and Fervour

Jeremy Mark Robinson

CRESCENT MOON

First published February 27, 1992. Second edition 2020.
© Jeremy Mark Robinson, 1992, 2020.

Design by Radiance Graphics
Set in Book Antiqua 11 on 13pt.

The right of Jeremy Mark Robinson to be identified as the author of this book has been asserted generally in accordance with sections 77 and 78 of the Copyright, Designs and Patents Act 1988.

All rights reserved. No part of this book may be reprinted or reproduced, stored in a retrieval system, or transmitted, in any form or by any means, electronic, mechanical, photocopying, recording or otherwise, without permission from the publisher.

British Library Cataloguing in Publication data available

ISBN-13 9781861717788 (Pbk)
ISBN-13 9781861717863 (Hbk)

Crescent Moon Publishing
P.O. Box 1312,
Maidstone, Kent
ME14 5XU, Great Britain
www.crmoon.com

CONTENTS

Acknowledgements • 9
Abbreviations • 11
Note On Texts • 13

Introduction • 19
1   Hall of Mirrors: *The Journal* • 25
2   The Philosophy of Fervour: *Fruits of the Earth* • 32
3   Art • 49
4   Fervour and Despair: *The Immoralist* • 63
5   Religion • 78
6   Philosophy • 89
7   Sensuality • 98
8   Love • 105
9   Joy • 114

Illustrations • 127
Notes • 136
Bibliography • 138

ACKNOWLEDGEMENTS

To Diane M. Moore, Geraldine Snowball, Mid-Kent College and West Kent College.

ABBREVIATIONS

F	*Fruits of the Earth*
I	*The Immoralist*
C	*The Counterfeiters*
SG	*Strait Is the Gate*
VC	*The Vatican Cellars*
If	*If It Die*
PS	*The Pastoral Symphony* and *Isabelle*
AW	*The Notebooks of André Walter*
C	*Corydon*
P	*Marshlands* (*Paludes*) and *Prometheus Misbound*
Et	*Et nunc mane in te* and *Intimate Journal*
Am	*Amyntas*
Pre	*Pretexts; Reflections On Literature and Morality*
OC	*Oeuvres completes*
J	*Journals 1889-1949*
J2	*Journal 1914-27*
AGDB	*The Selected Letters of André Gide and Dorothy Bussy*

NOTE ON TEXTS

I have used English translations of André Gide's work, in particular the Penguin editions of the fiction. The essential Gide shines through the translations, partly because Gide collaborated closely with his translators (these include Dorothy Bussy and Justin O'Brien).

ANDRÉ GIDE

André Gide in 1893

André Gide by Paul Laurens, 1924

INTRODUCTION

André Gide (1869-1951) is a writer's writer, a sophisticated, modern artist who progressed from French Symbolism to world-weary, international postmodernism. André Gide is a mass of contradictions, of paradoxes and tensions of all kinds. He is puritanical but pagan • an ascetic who adores sensuality • an atheist who yearns for God • a homosexual who all his life loved his wife, Madeleine Rondeaux (1867-1938) • he strived for objectivity while remaining one of the most introspective of writers • he needed the rainy domesticity of Normandy and the sun-baked wildness of North Africa • despite his prolific output he produced only one novel (in his sense of the term) • he is very much a part of the modern, European tradition (of Fyodor Dostoievsky, Friedrich Nietzsche, Rainer Maria Rilke, Gustave Flaubert, Arthur Rimbaud and Stéphane Mallarmé), while also standing outside it all, unclassifiable.

Born between the two different cultures of North and South France, André Gide was restless, always in motion. He is like Rainer Maria or Arthur Rimbaud in this respect: the wandering, alienated, detached, dispossessed, modern, European artist. At home nowhere – or everywhere. (We are all exiles, Julia Kristeva says).

All the contradictions of André Gide's personality are

explained and unified by one thing: he was an artist, first and foremost. Perhaps his most enduring quality is his constant unease and self-questioning. He never stayed with one belief for very long. The eternal qualities of André Gide were his love for his wife, Madeleine, his search for the purest kind of artistic form, his restlessness, his yearning for God, and his ever-changing formulations of ethical principles.

Like Albert Camus, Thomas Hardy, J.-K. Huysmans, and Oscar Wilde, André Gide was searching for an authentic way of living. He wanted to find out what 'livingness' was, what it meant to be alive, how best to live. His vision quest was as fevered as that of D.H. Lawrence, but it has all the hallmarks of the mystic's journey towards enlightenment. Gide's *Journals* and much of his fiction is one long Dark Night of the Soul out of traditional mysticism (*à la* Catholic mystics), in which everything is thrown into question. Doubt, pain, guilt, regret, yearning – Gide was racked by suffering as much as mystics such as St John of the Cross or Isaac of Nineveh. But Gide was no mystic, however. He was wary of mysticism. In the *Journal* and in the fiction, his mood swings from bitter, mature scepticism to adolescent, innocent belief. For sure Gide wanted to believe – in something – but the world dictated otherwise. The reality of being alive, of being in the world, and the world itself, are so often at odds with spiritual yearnings and inner questionings. The soul might be wanting one thing, but reality will dictate something else.

It's the passionate, artistic and philosophical André Gide we are interested in here. The fiction studied includes mainly *Fruits of the Earth, The Immoralist, Paludes, Strait Is The Gate, The Notebooks of André Walter, The Vatican Cellars, The Counterfeiters*, and one or two other pieces. There are good studies of André Gide's fiction available elsewhere, which take in all of his fiction, as well as studies of his complex artistry, life and views (for instance, see the

ANDRÉ GIDE

critical studies by David Walker, George Painter, Enid Starkie and D.L. Thomas). The aim here is to take a fresh look at *Les Nourritures Terrestres*, as well as the books closely associated with it: *The Immoralist, Pretexts, Amyntas, Paludes, Strait Is the Gate* and *André Walter*.

André Gide does have a remarkable range as an artist:
- the post-Rimbaudian blisses of *André Walter* and *Urien's Voyage*;
- the religious tragedies of *Strait Is The Gate* and *The Pastoral Symphony*;
- the Greek pieces, *Oedipus* and *Theseus*;
- the travel books, *Amyntas, Travels In the Congo, Dindiki,* and *Return From the U.S.S.R.*;
- the plays, *Saul, Bathsheba, King Candaules,* and *Philoctete*;
- the dense modern fiction, *The Counterfeiters,* and *The Vatican Cellars*;
- novellas such as *Isabelle, Geenevieve, Robert* and *The Immoralist*;
- the studies of Oscar Wilde, Fyodor Dostoievsky, and Michel de Montaigne;
- the essays and articles, *Pretexts, Miscellany, Angles of Incidence,* and *Imaginary Interviews*;
- the many collections of letters – to Rainer Maria Rilke, Edmund Gosse, Paul Claudel, etc;
- and not forgetting one of the key Gide works, the huge *Journal* (published in multiple volumes).

Something of a renaissance artist, André Gide is trying out so many different forms of communication. Much of his writing moves towards the letter or journal form. It is significant that he got so upset by the burning of his letters to his wife. His letters were very precious to him. Letter-writing was essential to his well-being, as with writers such as D.H. Lawrence, John Cowper

ANDRÉ GIDE

Powys, Rainer Maria Rilke and Henry Miller, other obsessive letter-authors. (Lawrence Durrell has his character Pursewarden's letters to his sister being burnt in his novel sequence *The Alexandria Quartet*, which I think is a reference to André Gide – and those letters, Pursewarden says in Durrell's 1950s novels, contained his best writing).

André Gide's prose comes out of the French literary tradition – out of Jean Racine, Molière, Michel de Montaigne, Francois Marie Arouet (Voltaire), Stendhal, Charles Baudelaire and Stéphane Mallarmé – moving on through Paul Valéry, Paul Claudel, Albert Camus, Jean-Paul Sartre, and Alain Robbe-Grillet. Yet philosophically, Gide has much in common with the Neoplatonists of the ancient Near East, with Plato and Aristotle in Ancient Greece, with Gnosticism and Catharism, and with Buddhism in India and China.

Much has been made of the influence of Friedrich Nietzsche on André Gide (Nietzsche is of course one of the biggest influences on writers and artists in the 20th century – so many writers have cited Nietzsche as an influence, continuing to the present day, among writers such as Julia Kristeva and Luce Irigaray. French *avant garde* writers in particular adore Nietzsche).

We can see the influence of German Idealist and Romantic writers and thinkers, such as Johann Wolfgang von Goethe, Novalis, Friedrich von Schlegel and Immanuel Kant on André Gide. Arthur Schopenhauer was an early love of Gide's: both Gide and Schopenhauer are concerned with issues such as ethics, melancholy, irony, belief, education, being, æsthetics, intellect, sin, art, courage and freedom. There's a quasi-Buddhist element of renunciation and asceticism in Schopenhauer's philosophy which would appeal to Gide. And Schopenhauer is another of those highly intellectual, well-read and modern, European philosophers who fit in so well with modernist literature, particularly that of Europe in the early and middle twentieth century (as well as Existentialism, of course). Some classic Schopenhauer quotes:

> A man can be himself only so long as he is alone, and if he does not love solitude, he will not love freedom, for it is only when he is alone that he is really free.
>
> •
>
> We forfeit three-quarters of ourselves in order to be like other people.
>
> •
>
> So the problem is not so much to see what nobody has yet seen, as to think what nobody has yet thought concerning that which everybody sees.

André Gide is not a philosopher, though, and does not have a developed 'system'. He is in a state of Heraclitean flux, more in Strife than in the state of Love, in the Empedoclean sense.

Both André Gide and Arthur Schopenhauer founded their ethics upon intensity. 'Intellect is a magnitude', wrote Schopenhauer in his *Essays* (125). The Gidean self loves intelligence, and is always intelligent, even when it harks after a primitive sense of being (in the characters of Lafcadio in *The Vatican Cellars* and Michel in *The Immoralist*, etc). The Northern European spirit, as exemplified by Fyodor Dostoievsky, Johann Wolfgang von Goethe, Friedrich Nietzsche and Arthur Schopenhauer, is found in much of Gide's art. Despite his love of the Southern European way of life, he remains a Northern European artist.

CHAPTER ONE

HALL OF MIRRORS

THE *JOURNAL/ JOURNALS*

A central image in André Gide's work is of the writer looking into a mirror and writing about himself. A self-portrait in prose. Gide's work is full of self-reflexivity, mirror-imaging, and *mise-en-âbyme*, all kinds of notes on the soul, the psyche, self-analysis leading to self-loathing, narcissism and the *Journal* (the technical, literary phrase *mise-en-âbyme* can only be expressed in French it seems – it just doesn't sound as cool in English).

The world is all projection, ultimately, in André Gide's art: everything is preparation, everything can go into the *Journal* and the fiction. The question of the content of the *Journal*, of what to put in one's most sacred creation, weighs Gide down. His *Journal* is a mirror, but a very selective mirror. There is mediation and editing and a limitation imposed on confession. When will Gide become sick of himself? How much can you write about yourself?

André Gide was so aware of the nature of writing, above all

other arts. He knew and explored how much of the self there is in a work of art. His books are self-questioning and intrapersonal communication, taken to poetic extremes. Art out of life, yes, and perhaps his characters are self-portraits. Gide has a spacious soul, full of a multiplicity of selves.

In many ways, André Gide's *Journal* is his best, most accomplished creation (and a work he cherished). Gide is very like Anaïs Nin – her *Journals* stand at the centre of her creative work. She too lived in Paris; was surrounded by creative people; had unorthodox views of sexuality; used psychology, dreams, etc; drew upon French literature; aimed for richness; was sensual; and wrote in a lyrical manner (but that description could apply to any French *avant garde* writer, couldn't it? They are all 'radical', 'sensual', 'unorthodox', 'psychological', 'bohemian', etc. It's *de rigeur* for a French author).

But André Gide holds back much material from his *Journal*: he scrupulously selects the material, revealing only what he wishes. He is very self-conscious, very aware of writing for posterity, for future audiences. He is restrained in his public self, shy to the point of being painful. He feels embarrassment keenly. He lets known his fears, homosexuality, sleeplessness and discomfort, but it's all done in a tightly controlled manner. Gide is thinking, even in the early 1890s, of future publication, and how he will be viewed by others. This entry from January 5, 1902 is typical.

> I am no good except when alone. In a group it's not so much the others that bore and annoy me; it's myself. (J, 58)

Typical self-hatred and self-awareness here, and a classic, Gidean approach to sociability. André Gide aches for this guilty admission to be read by someone else. His friends will say, 'oh, so that's why André was so strange in company'. Literary critics will comment: 'Gide's self-loathing forms the emotional basis for the

ANDRÉ GIDE

Existential displacement of his fiction.'

André Gide is often painfully self-conscious. He seems to be a stylist, a poseur. He strikes self-conscious attitudes in his work. Art is foregrounded. Even in the fiction he is aware of the processes of creation, and makes sure everyone else knows too.

In *The Counterfeiters,* he writes (via his narrator) as if he's making a few books at the same time. He is always aware of the literary possibilities of his works. He writes of ideas, but he is not an 'ideas novelist' like, say, Aldous Huxley or H.G. Wells. He is a moralist, something of a social prophet, like D.H. Lawrence or Leo Tolstoy, although he keeps this tendency in check. There are few passages in Gide's art where he really lets go. Lorenzo lets himself go often, like Walt Whitman – it all tumbles out. Not Gide. Apart from the eulogies in *Fruits of the Earth* and *André Walter,* there are few passionate flights in Gide's work. So self-reflexive he is, so detached and studiedly ironic. He writes into a mirror, in the same way that Egon Schiele drew his anguished self-portraits into mirrors. All art is self-portrait, commented Jean Cocteau, and Gide would certainly agree with that.

André Gide's fiction is more of a self-portrait than most novelists' fiction, but he doesn't load his books with his ego like, say, Henry Miller or James Joyce. Gide is not a full-blown persona in his art. He is not a 'heroic' artist, like Michelangelo Buonarroti or Ernest Hemingway. He is there, rather, like V.S. Naipaul – a presence, diffuse at times, yet always focussed.

For André Gide is sharp: he is clever, in control, but restrained. He does not show off his intelligence and wide-reading and learning, as John Cowper Powys was prone to do at every opportunity. No, Gide is self-restrictive. He is not effusive, like Johann Wolfgang von Goethe, but sophisticated, like Stendhal.

The refined, world-weary irony of a Stendhal or an E.M. Forster is not easy to attain. It usually shows through as pretension and affectation. But André Gide is authentic. He is the genuine article – an artist. Writers such as E.M. Forster and Evelyn Waugh come across as much more affected and strained than Gide. Gide doesn't seem to strain, to over-reach himself. He stays within his limits. He knows his boundaries.

André Gide's province is the human animal shifted only slightly out of its usual niche. Gide's characters are always on the edge of collapse, or danger, but he keeps them on the respectable side of insanity. Gide is not Fyodor Dostoievsky or Arthur Rimbaud. Real madness would terrify him, one thinks. He is respectable, and respectful. He is a gentle kind of rebel, nowhere near as polemical as Albert Camus or Gertrude Stein.

André Gide's is gentle polemic, yet he too wants to throw away much of contemporary culture. Modern Christianity, for example, is not his religion, and neither is it D.H. Lawrence's or Henry Miller's: and, like Lawrence and Miller, Gide is a polemical and political writer. He campaigns in his fiction, like Thomas Hardy did, for increased compassion. Both Hardy and Gide are Buddhist in their urges towards a human-scale cult of compassion. Gide is less conservative than Hardy, however.

Much of André Gide's fiction tells of a shift in a life-stance stemming from some deep experience. Thomas Hardy tries to patch things up, while Gide, like Arthur Rimbaud, would rather sweep them away and grow something new. Like Rimbaud, Gide is anarchic, something of a 'romantic anarchist' (Michael Moorcock's term). Like Bruce Chatwin, Gide searched for 'the miraculous', for the Extra Something that would enrich life.

Like Bertrand Russell, André Gide is egalitarian. He wants to improve the lot of humankind. He acknowledges the many pains of human life ('all life is sorrowful', say the Buddhist texts), but he can see room for societal improvements on many levels. God is dead, said Friedrich Nietzsche, and Gide tried to find an authentic, modern-age belief system. His fervent, private Protestantism gave him a need for a God of a kind. He searched for God, like Thomas Hardy and Ingmar Bergman, but so rarely found him. Disappointment and disaffection is the lot of the modern human, it seems. Injustices of all kinds are everywhere, as Albert Camus pointed out.

There are no easy solutions, André Gide knew that. He was not over-zealous in his sociological pronouncements, like D.H. Lawrence, but was often no less incisive. The answers Gide provided were usually ambiguous. Part of him yearned to be a teacher, a prophet, a guru in the mould of Menelcas of *Fruits of the Earth*, but he is uncomfortable to take up such a position for long. He is restless. Part of him wants to be consoled like a child, while another part yearns to be in erotic love like a teenager. Another part wants to travel the open road like a young drifter, while yet another part desires a soft middle-aged bout of contemplation in some Andalusian rose garden. And another part of Gide would like to be the smiling Buddha, sitting cross-legged on a lotus-shaped throne, ready to receive eager, young boys intent on initiation into the mysteries of life.

André Gide plays each of these roles in his fiction, letters and *Journal*. He moves swiftly between them. His fictional characters reflect his varied desires. It is easy in a Gide book to pick out his archetypes, just as it is in the fiction of Aldous Huxley or Joseph Conrad. There are the usual Gidean, illegitimate, young gay men; the wise, old pederasts; the sad, married women; the sin-obsessed, young women; and the sensualists, etc.

Persona upon persona – André Gide's fiction is full of them. It's obvious what's going on with Gide's characters, except, perhaps, in *Les Faux-Monnayeurs*, when the characters are subordinated to the complex self-reflexivity, the literary architecture of the *mise-en-âbyme*. Multiple personas, then: extensions of the Gidean self.

The form of each book itself it another element. For André Gide's work is never formless. He condenses his art, he hones it,

ANDRÉ GIDE

sharpens it up. His mind is sharp, and delicate – light and limpid: musically, it's Fréderic Chopin not Ludwig von Beethoven.

Form plays an important role. One of André Gide's great strengths is his concision. Only his *Journal* is a weighty tome, unlike the large volumes of such prolix writers as John Cowper Powys, Charles Dickens or Fyodor Dostoievsky. Gide is a delight to read because of this, these short works. Gide hates waste. As with Ursula Le Guin's work, most of his works have no padding. Only the *Journal* allows meandering.

In general, André Gide's output is precise and concise. Clarity of thought is a premium with him. He wants a clear read, as he says many times in his *Journal*. He wants a good night's sleep, so he can think clearly. He doesn't like having his mind contaminated with bad experiences. Places as well as people fatigue him.

André Gide is restless like Arthur Rimbaud: he keeps moving about the world. Gide writes his *Journal* from a large number of places. You get the same sense of dissatisfaction and endless travelling in the letters of Rimbaud, or D.H. Lawrence. These artists couldn't keep still. They would have died, stifled in one city, one place. Rimbaud had to get out of Charleville and France, and Lawrence had to escape from Nottinghamshire and England; and Gide, after his early, North African experience, couldn't stay still for too long. Similarly with Lawrence Durrell, who left England for Corfu and Paris and the Greek islands. This restlessness gives an edge to Gide's work, keeps it fresh.

CHAPTER TWO

THE PHILOSOPHY OF FERVOUR

FRUITS OF THE EARTH/

LES NOURRITURES TERRESTRES

The pervading themes, images and motifs of *Fruits of the Earth* (*Les Nourritures Terrestres*, 1897), André Gide's early, visionary novel, written when he was 28, are of asceticism, purity, renunciation, joy, sensualism, nostalgia, travel, homoeroticism, pedagogy and growth. The book aims to teach, to teach Nathaniel, the hero of the piece. The narrator was in turn taught by the guru Menalcas, who at the end of *Fruits of the Earth* sails away.

The narrator is a poet, traveller, bohemian and sensualist. He lives from day to day, on the wing. He aches for freedom, choice and deep experiences.

The overall dynamic of *Fruits of the Earth* is *desire*; desire pervades the book. Desire for experiences, for sensations, for journeys, for places, for certain people. The desire is for the enrichment of life, but in an ascetic, esoteric sense. The narrator advocates a total immersion in desires, in sensations, in the thicknesses of life. At the same time, taking his cue from the *Gospels*, he desires purification.

Desire!

It envelops *Fruits of the Earth*, and is the driving force behind the work. The book is drenched, most of all, with the desire of the narrator to have his thirst quenched. Thirsts of all kinds suffuse the book, especially the thirst for water. Not a flood, but a cool draft of pure water from an oasis in the desert.

There is hunger here too: hunger for deep experiences, for the Magreb, for travel, for the electric caresses of young boys. Nathaniel, says the Gidean persona in *Fruits of the Earth*, dive in deep into life while you can. Dive in deep, without thinking, without planning. Spontaneity is the key. All Gidean splendours must be spontaneous. He wanders, sees ecstasy by the roadside, and dives into it.

Desire and detachment. Both work together, but desire comes first: the Western materialistic, pornographic desire to possess, to experience, and to re-possess in memory, as with Constantin Cavafy and Lawrence Durrell. André Gide is a poet of memory, of nostalgia. He wallows in erotic and exotic thoughts. Not of the grand, event-filled, historic past, but of his own highly individual experiences. His life becomes his art. The *Journal* shows this time and time again.

Desire: from Plato to Sigmund Freud and Jacques Lacan the desire-and-lack model has been central to Western sexual metaphysics: in this negative model, one is doomed to a desire for more and more consumption, which leads to dissatisfaction. Freudian-Lacanian desire can never be satisfied: dissatisfaction is built-in.

Desire is never annihilated: for the philosopher Georg

Wilhelm Hegel, only another desire can satisfy desire and also perpetuate it. Desire thus desires more desire (this has a vivid expression in late capitalist consumerism, where it is always the next commodity that will truly satisfy and stop the hunger for more objects. But it never happens).

Far better to see desire, as Elizabeth Grosz does in "Refiguring Lesbian Desire", as a positive force, one which (following Benedictus de Spinoza and Friedrich Nietzsche as opposed to G.W.F. Hegel and Sigmund Freud) makes connections and alliances. Instead of regarding desire as a repetitive search for something to make up for a central, gaping loss, it is seen as a force of production and creative assemblage, not fantasmatic, but real (in L. Doan, 75).

This view of desire (in the work of Nietzsche, Spinoza, Gilles Deleuze and Félix Guattari), is also that of the French feminists Hélène Cixous and Luce Irigaray. Desire becomes not yearning but actualization, actions, creation: instead of a Lacanian lack, desire becomes primary. As Cixous says: 'my desires have invented new desires' (in E. Marks, 246).

André Gide likes to be on display, but he is careful about the sides he shows. He edits meticulously his art. He reveals only what he wants to reveal. He is self-conscious in a youthful, almost immature way, as if he's hiding something, like a painfully embarrassed teenager. What does he have to hide? Not his homosexuality – he revealed that in his book *Corydon* (1925), which had a limited publication and a tiny readership, and earlier in *Fruits of the Earth*, and *The Immoralist*. (*Corydon* is regarded as the book where Gide 'came out' as a writer. *Corydon* was a series of dialogues about homosexuality and pederasty, not fiction featuring homoerotic acts. There was considerable anxiety, though, about how *Corydon* would be received, and how it might cause offence; hence the guarded way in which it was published). However, there are hints of persecution in Gide's work, which often surround the issue of homosexuality in fiction – persecution that's linked, as ever, to Christian religion.

André Gide reveals himself piece by piece. He knows exactly what he's doing, word for word. His art is so intricately manipulated. He is the consummate performer. *Les Nourritures Terrestres* is one of the rare moments when he lets go (which's one of the marks of it being a work of Gide's youth).

In *Fruits of the Earth*, he becomes vivacious, exhilarated. He is Rimbaudian, Baudelairean, Huysmansean, Wildean, Decadent. He exalts the sensual life. He dives into sensations like J.-K. Huysmans' des Esseintes in *À Rebours/ Against Nature* (one of the key books of the *avant garde* of the *fin-de-siècle* and Gide's formative years).

It is a religious book, *Les Nourritures Terrestres*. It opens with an exhortation to God (p. 17). God, says André Gide's narrator, is everywhere. Already Gide sounds more Islamic than Christian. God is in everything, but do not let everything distract you from God (17). The Islamic Sufi mystics say similar things, such as Mansur Al-Hallaj, Abu Hamid Muhammad ibn Muhammad Al-Ghazzali, Ab Hamid bin Ab Bakr Ibrahim (Attar) and Jalal al-Din Muhammad Rumi. The central tenets of Islam are that there is one God and that is Allah and Muhammad is his prophet. From this diamond-hard unity everything else follows. Islamic religion emphasis daily ritual and prayer, rigorous self-discipline, the pilgrimage to Mecca, fervour, and mysticism (embodied in Sufism and Sufic poetry).

The next stage is the ontological un-learning – to forget one's deeply enculturated self. Morals are jettisoned in favour of a new system (that is a non-system). Life will be passionate (of course). The initiate must now set off into the country of the Unknown. Every self is alone, and makes their own pathway through the psychic Unknown.

How close André Gide is here to Buddhism, to Western

magicke, and to modern thinkers such as Joseph Campbell.

All this is on page 17 of *Fruits of the Earth*, the first page of Book One. Before this is the prologue – a couple of paragraphs in which the Gidean narrator exhorts his initiate Nathaniel to throw away his book after he's read it:

And when you have read me, throw this book away – and go out. (13)

'Go out' – this is typical of André Gide. He does not mean 'read the book then meditate for a couple of years', he means: 'Go outside – do something with your new knowledge, your new state of being'.

Be consumed, then be transcendent. Dive in deep, then soar up high, this is what André Gide is saying. 'Throw away the book' – this cry is taken up in the Envoi of *Fruits of the Earth*:

Leave me; now you are in my way. (136)

The narrator has been learning too. Now his pupil, Nathaniel, is in his way. Growth must continue to have its path, its freedom. Give me space now, the Gidean soul says. All things must grow, must be in a state of continuous refinement.

Before this opening section there is a quote from John Milton. There are other quotes – from Johnann Wolfgang von Goethe, Virgil and Shams al-Din Muhammad Hafiz. Milton's quote is 'Food, not of angels...' There is food in here, in this book – luscious fruit, no less. But it is not angelic, nor is it dæmonic. It is, purely and simply, fruit from the Earth.

So, after the opening page, André Gide widens his polemic. It now turns out that the book is composed of short pieces, sometimes a page or two, but more often short paragraphs. Some sections are just a line long. It is Rimbaudian prose-poetry (developed from Rimbaud's *Illuminations*), and also reminds me of Gertrude Stein at times, as well as Rimbaud. Gide's tone is didactic, but gentle; strident but quietly insistent. He teaches, or tries to teach. He teaches *fervour*.

This is a magnificent line, when you come to it, after a couple of pages. It is the central message of the whole work:

Nathanael, je t'enseignerai la ferveur.
(Nathaniel, I will teach you fervour.)
(*Fruits of the Earth*, page 18)

Fervour – the fervour of desire, the fervour of the yearning, burning, aching to have thirsts quenched – this is the driving energy behind the 1897 book.

Follow – André Gide says – but follow the light that is inside you. Pure Oriental philosophy this. The light is inside you, it is your own way, I am here to awaken you to it merely – I cannot find it for you. And the means, says Gide, are many. But love and poetry feature highly.

All this is very subjective, naturally. 'God is what lies ahead of you', says the guru Menalcas. And André Gide says: 'Let the importance lie in your look, not in the thing you look at.' (18)

Les Nourritures Terrestres is a poem to fervour, to a fervent philosophy of life. Much of the time Gide speaks in maxims, in fables, in epigrams. Here is a selection:

MAXIMS FROM *FRUITS OF THE EARTH*

Nathaniel, I will teach your fervour (18)

All fervour consumed me with love – consumed me deliciously (18)

Melancholy is nothing but abated fervour (19)

Let every moment renew your vision (25)

You must make a bonfire in your heart, Nathaniel, of all our books (26)

ANDRÉ GIDE

Nathaniel, let every one of your emotions be an intoxication to you (32)

The only wisdom I want to teach you is life (36)

Nathaniel, I want to bring you to life (36)

Nathaniel, here is all the warmth of my soul – take it (37)

My happiness is made of fervour (63)

We can never strip our souls so bare as to leave enough room in them for love (80)

The present possession of THIS always came to me as rapture (82)

Nathaniel, I will speak to you of everything (93)

This is the day and we believe in it (106)

Nathaniel, ah! satisfy your joy while it gladdens your soul (126)

Ah! if only we were not wakened into life again by a fresh onslaught of desire (129)

Do not think your truth can be found by anyone else (136)

You do not wonder as you should of the astounding miracle of your life (141)

With mind and hand I brush aside all intercepting veils, so that there shall be nothing before me but what is brilliant and bare (146)

No sooner am I awake than astonishment fills me that I exist, and my wonder is unceasing (153)

It is renunciation that brings all virtue to perfection (156)

The true Christian is he whom pure water suffices to intoxicate (168)

I am amazed at everything on this earth (175)

ANDRÉ GIDE

It is now and in this world that we must live (213)

And so it begins, two sorts of prose in *Fruits of the Earth*: the poetry of experience, action and sensation; then the reflection upon this experience, the ideas and thoughts.

André Gide has not, though, rushed through Africa with a notebook, writing it all down as he lives it. No, he writes it from a distance – looking back (or down) from Northern France to North Africa. The Magreb has taken hold of him, but he doesn't write there, he writes in his homeland.

Other choice places are mentioned or inflected in the text of *Fruits of the Earth*: Florence, Seville, Paris. These places are noted, in the style of a personal journal, with dates at the head of each paragraph, as if this is a (spiritual) journal only just written, the ink still wet, the blood still hot.

Once in motion, the pattern of the book is laid out: it is Mediterranean: Tunis, Malta, Naples, Seville. The favoured season is Summer – the book overflows with images of Summer, of heat, of exotic locations, of lassitude, of travel:

Summer! golden ooze; profusion; glory of increased light; immense overflowing of love! (116)

There are all kinds of bohemian, stylized, sensual images in *Fruits of the Earth*: of the deserts and oases and caravans of dreams; of hot noons and hushed twilights; of Renaissance and Islamic cities; Autumns; journeys; flowers; water; colours. *Fruits of the Earth* is a scrapbook of desires and sensations:

Nathaniel, I will teach you fervour. Our acts are attached to us as its glimmer is to phosphorous. They consume us, it is true, but they make our splendour.
 And if our souls have been of any worth, it is because they have burnt more ardently than others. Great fields, washed in the

whiteness of dawn, I have seen you; blue lakes, I have bathed in your waters – and to every caress of the laughing breeze I have smiled back an answer – this is what I shall never tire of telling you, Nathaniel. I will teach you *fervour*. (20)

Light is exalted many times in *Fruits of the Earth* (for example on page 152); water and springs appear throughout; touches are ached for; the seashore (27); bodies; plants and stone. André Gide writes of touch thus:

Among all the joys of the senses it was those I envied. (85)

He goes on to describe a tree and the experience of water. Water and light and heat – prime experiences, prime realities of the world, of being in the world – suffuse the book. Springs are eulogized (pp. 31, 43, 114), as are oases (116). The poet's joy is, he says: 'nothing but glorified LIGHT' (44).

Les Nourritures Terrestres is a summary of all the sensual delights exalted in poetry since the Ancient Greeks – from Plato and Sappho to Friedrich Hölderlin and Arthur Rimbaud:

Extraordinaire ivresse des crépuscules d'été sur les places, quand il fait encore tres clair et que pourtant on n'a plus d'ombres. Exaltation très speciale.
(Strange intoxications of Summer twilights in the open places of the town, when it's still very light and yet there are no shadows. A very special kind of excitement. [40])

André Gide's narrator in *Fruits of the Earth* sings of the senses. He is alive to all kinds of impulses. In Book VI he lists each of his sense's experiences: his ears hear water and wind; his eyes see sunlight and trees; his flesh feels damp moss (105). For Gide this is all of life – plus his self. He is not just a 'rendezvous of sensations' (105). There is his self too, his soul, the re-born being.

Arthur Rimbaud, in his extraordinary book of poetry *Illuminations*, described his sensory experiences in a similar

ANDRÉ GIDE

manner. This, from his *Illuminations*, could be inserted into André Gide's *Fruits of the Earth* with no changes necessary:

> Assez vu. La vision s'est rencontrée à tous les airs.
>   Assez eu. Rumeurs des villes, le soir, et au soleil, et toujours.
>   Assez connu. Les arrêts de la vie. – O Rumeurs et Visions!
>   Départ dans l'affection et le bruit neufs!
>
> (Seen enough. The vision meets itself in every air.
>   Had enough. Rumours of towns, in the evening, and in sunlight, and always.
>   Known enough. The halts of life. – Oh sounds and visions!
>   Departure into new affection and new sounds.)
> (From 'Departure')
>
> La plaque du foyer noir, de réels soleils des grèves: ah! puits des magies; seule vue d'aurore, cette fois.
>
> (The plaque of the black earth, real suns of the shore: ah! well of magic; a solitary sight of the sunrise, this time.)
> (From 'Vigils' – translations by Andrew Jary)

André Gide's 1897 book has a life of its own outside of Arthur Rimbaud's poetry, although his debt to Rimbaud is not a minor one. The sensual poetry is the best part of *Fruits of the Earth*. Like Paul Verlaine and Rimbaud, Gide excels in short but evocative descriptions of his sensations. He writes of the beauties of Florence, Rome, Amalfi, Syracuse, Tunis, Malta and Blidah (Book VII). He writes of the 'rainy, domesticated land' of Northern France (79). He sings of fruit (pp. 31, 65, 88). He writes of industrial towns (103).

The last Book of *Les Nourritures Terrestres* (VIII) finds the poet in Paris, looking back nostalgically, yearning and remembering his many past pleasures.

Fruits of the Earth is didactic. André Gide hopes to teach with it. Nathaniel is the younger incarnation of Gide. He is invoked many times. There are three selves: Gide in the middle;

ANDRÉ GIDE

Nathaniel as the young initiate; and the older, wiser Menalcas, who is something of a Tiresias figure. It is a Classical (Greek) configuration. Gide plays at being each one (an author is always every character in their novels, not only the narrator. And Gide is Nathaniel and Menalcas as well as the narrator, as well as Gide the writer commenting upon them).

Nathaniel is André Gide's heart's desire. He wants him so much. But Nathaniel is a part of himself. Most of all, Gide wants to make love to himself, to the best, the youngest, the freshest part of himself, his Nathaniel. So he loads all the weight of his experience onto Nathaniel:

> Do not try, Nathaniel, to find God here or there – but everywhere. (17)

> ...And so, Nathaniel, you're like the man who should follow as his guide the light he holds in his own hand. (18)

> No, not sympathy, Nathaniel – love. (18)

> I should like to draw near you and make you love me. (19)

> Nathaniel, let your waiting be not even a longing, but simply a welcoming (25)

> A bonfire, Nathaniel, of all our books!!! (27)

> Nathaniel, I want to bring you to life. (36)

> Nathaniel, here is all the warmth of my soul – take it. (37)

> Nathaniel, I will speak to you of everything. (93)

The poet has been reborn into life and wants to share it, and to pass on his experience and learning. Written in illness, *Fruits of the Earth* shows clearly André Gide's joy on re-awakening to the experiences of being alive. He sleeps like a chrysalis, then awakens (22). Menalcas is partly a catalyst for the poet's rebirth:

ANDRÉ GIDE

> I fell ill; I travelled, I met Menalcas, and my marvellous
> convalescence was a palingenesis. I was born again with a new self,
> in a new country, and amongst things which were absolutely fresh.
> (24)

All these things are bound up together – André Gide's favourite time of day is the morning, when the Earth is fresh, waiting to sail into another day (and the future). Gide's favourite time of life is youth. He loves freshness, youth, energy. He is here reborn – this is like yearning for transcendence, for moving up and out and beyond everything.

So, partly because of his love of freshness and youth he speaks of moments: 'Nathaniel, I must speak to you of moments. Do you realize the power of their presence?' (37). This is mystical, the evocation of the timeless moment, found in most world religions and in modern poets such as Rainer Maria Rilke, T.S. Eliot, Paul Claudel, Robert Graves and Paul Éluard, among others.

Bliss is now, of course. We all live in the present. The present moment is all we have. So let's live (existence consisting of moments has affinities with the British scientist Julian Barbour, who reckons that time doesn't exist, but moments do. Chronological time is created from humans' sense of memory, Barbour reckons, but time doesn't actually exist – there are only moments; Gide I'm sure would embrace this scientific notion).

Thus André Gide writes: 'I lived in an almost perpetual state of passionate wonder.' (28) Always live in the present, and always be hungry, as Gide says:

> The most beautiful thing I have known on earth,
> Ah! Nathaniel, is my hunger. (32)

The theme of thirsts and hungers being satisfied runs

ANDRÉ GIDE

throughout the book:

> The greatest joys of my senses
> Have been the thirsts I have quenched. (95)

Big hungers, big thirsts, big living in the moment. Desires, sensations, satisfactions – the Gidean persona wants them all, and preferably all at once.

André Gide is pedagogical – he desires to teach, and he desires to be a teacher. He wants to instruct, to inform, to exchange important information. His real province is pedagogy – teaching, and he most wants to teach ways of living. He is a writer of ethics, of actions – he did this or that, etc. He speaks of writing lying down, sitting up, or standing (J, 35), but not what he is writing. He sits, stands, walks, travels – he is always in motion (or he appears to be). He is ethical: he says do this, do that.

Ways of living fascinate him most – think of North Africa. It's the way people live in North Africa that makes it fascinating, not the landscape. This is why André Gide went there – and why so many other writers did (including Paul Bowles, Lawrence Durrell and William Burroughs).

In *Fruits of the Earth*, André Gide's narrator tells Nathaniel to throw away the book, to leave him and to live. He is a Buddhist, a writer aching to become a sage, a mentor, a guru – he wants to be Swami Gide! Gide the Guru! The man who knows everything. He aches for transcendence, to transcend his present situation. Being human hurts him. Transformation: the butterfly and the cocoon: his writing creates a cocoon in which his many alter-egos can be born, re-born and re-incarnated. Birth and the dropping away of all unnecessary things.

The Gidean narrator advocates purity, asceticism, transformation, ethics, methodology and precision.

Fruits of the Earth is very much a product of its time – the

ANDRÉ GIDE

1890s, the era of Decadence and Symbolist art. It is the book of the Symbolist era, really, much more than J.-K. Huysmans' *À Rebours*. Gide's book is much more creative: it is a workbook, a sourcebook, full of suggestions of ways of living. Read the book, then throw it away, but *do it*. Gide and his narrator want Nathaniel to do it, to really do it. Nathaniel is the future Gidean self, and Menalcas is the old, decayed self, to be rejected but also cherished. Both the old world and the new world are valuable. But for Gide the most precious stuff is the future, embodied in youth and fresh mornings. Mornings, I salute you, says Gide (and we know just what he means. You have to salute mornings).

André Gide adores mornings. They mean new prospects, new possibilities, new people, and, best of all, new places. An early rising means an early departure for the Gidean writer or self. He desires motion, being on the road, moving on, never stopping: he did this in his books, each one different from the one before. Gide likes to know that soon he'll be travelling again – it is a common feeling, not bound to particular cultures or ages.

> I go out as soon as it is morning; I walk; I look at nothing and see everything; a marvellous symphony of subconscious sensations is formed and harmonized within me. (112)

Come into the morning, says André Gide in *Les Nourritures Terrestres* (106). Let's go. And *be hungry*. Gide loves hunger, his own hunger. He is drunk and he is hungry. He worships his own hunger (32). Be hungry, be drunk, be open for experiences. Intoxication is a goal. Let your hunger deepen until the intoxication increases.

Hunger does this: all the senses are sharpened, and even water can taste delicious. Gide says that water should be enough to intoxicate oneself, as it did with the saints. Let the simplest events become blissful.

This is André Gide the martyr, the mystic, the saint talking here. Everything is exaggerated, taken to its extreme. This extremism is a hallmark of artists of the 1880s and 1890s: Gustave Moreau, Arthur Rimbaud, Vincent van Gogh, Jean Deville and Oscar Wilde. Colours are not merely bright, they are radiant. Perfumes are not vague whiffs but rich scents. Textures are not dull but luxurious. Think of visual artists such as Félicien Rops, Odilon Redon, Aubrey Beardsley and the Pre-Raphaelites, or, among writers, Friedrich Nietzsche, Fyodor Dostoievsky and Walt Whitman.

But *Fruits of the Earth*, as André Gide says, was a reaction against Symbolism and the literature of the time (OC, 13, 440). The book is a poem to *la ferveur*. It aims to create a mythology of *ferveur*, a philosophy of fervent living.

Nostalgia plays a large part in this creation. Even in the earlier book of *Fruits of the Earth*, written only a year or two after the North African experiences that inspired the work, André Gide is deeply nostalgic. But the *Later Fruits of the Earth* is very nostalgic. As Gide wrote:

> Even today I suffer a kind of nostalgia for that mystical and fiery climate that once exalted my being; *I have never recovered the fervour of my adolescence.* (J, 513; my italics)

Fruits of the Earth cleverly orchestrates its invented reader, Nathaniel, the guru Menalcas, and the disaffected narrator, in its pursuit of fervent nostalgia.

Ferveur, volupté, disponibilité, désir – these are the key concepts that André Gide wants to communicate. The book rides on youthful desire. In 1923, Gide wrote: 'When desire subsides so does my whole being' (J, 366).

The external movement in *Fruits of the Earth* is away from towns, families and society, towards travel, restlessness, the desert, cafés and the company of artists, vagabonds, young boys, people on the fringes of society. The movement internally is towards self-denial, and rebirth.

Growth is one of André Gide's main preoccupations, in all his art. Progress is essential he maintains in *Fruits of the Earth*: 'I cannot wish for a state that is not progressive' (F, 201). Transcendence must be obtained at all costs. 'Man is in process of becoming', says the narrator of *Fruits of the Earth*, in his most Nietzschean mode (208).

André Gide has great faith in transcendence, in becoming. Becoming, not being, that is Gide's way (Friedrich Nietzsche had written about the process of becoming – Nietzsche's a philosopher who was himself definitely in a state of constant becoming, never attaining being). Gide would prefer quiescent beingness, but it does not work for him.

The *Journal* shows how restless Gide was, how eternally dissatisfied. 'Even in regard to oneself it is essential not to come to a stop', he remarked (J, 739). At one point Gide says he only wanted to be loved (everybody can relate to that!), but agreed to wait until another life for this love, even though he didn't believe in an afterlife (702, 756).

Les Nourritures Terrestres was a book that André Gide had to write – it was the crystallization of his philosophy of fervour, but, once he'd written it, he transcended it, and left it all behind him (of course – the writing of the book is the means of self-transcendence). It was a stage in his growth as an artist, but an important one. Although he tried to play down the significance of the book in the later years, it is pure Gide.

CHAPTER THREE

ART

I invent a novelist, whom I make my central figure; and the subject of the book, if you must have one, is just that very struggle between what reality offers him and what he himself desires to make of it.

André Gide, *The Counterfeiters* (pp. 168-9)

André Gide's artistic credo is summed up in this phrase from the early work *Paludes*: 'Once we take up an idea, we must carry it to the very end' (P, 86). This idea is very much of its time, this desire to push everything to extremes. It is not a new idea: think of the Pyramids, a concept exaggerated to titanic proportions, or the vanities and insanities of the Medicis and the Popes in Renaissance Italy.

Be extreme – this is one of André Gide's guiding artistic precepts. It is part of his ethical attempt to be pure. As Edouardo puts it in *The Counterfeiters*: 'in art, as in everything else, purity is the only thing I care about' (C, 71). Purity is an obsession in *Fruits of the Earth*.

The plastic metaphor or manifestation in André Gide's work

is water, free-flowing water. Freedom is essential for him. He hates being tied down to one train of thought. He must keep mobile. He writes that 'the moment I am delivered of one book I fly to the opposite extremity of my self' (If, 207). Be free, be spontaneous: 'I like chance, adventure, the unknown; I like not to be where I am expected to be' (ib., 208).

André Gide likes to be chameleon-like. He likes to be a shape-shifter, a writer who can dance into many different roles. Lafcadio in *The Vatican Cellars* prizes 'above all things the free possession of his soul' (56). Prisons kill, and Gide, like Albert Camus, fights against all kinds of ontological oppressions and traps. Edouardo in *The Counterfeiters* needs escape, like his creator (C, 68).

Fruits of the Earth was the first book by André Gide I read, and it coloured the rest of his work for me, as often with the first work one encounters of an artist. Reading *Strait Is the Gate* first, for instance, would give you a different Gide, a different experience.

The more we read André Gide, the more it becomes clear that he is a deceptively complex writer. This is because for him, in his own mind, the concepts of freedom, spontaneity, purity, ethics, identity, escape, etc, are all bound up together. For him, ethics are æsthetic, in a similar way that for Ludwig Wittgenstein (1961) mathematics and ethics were transcendent.

In other words, André Gide sees everything as bound up together, but intuitively and experientially. He is not a methodical, logical philosopher. He is no scientist. He sees the world as a poet. Design and form are part, therefore, of moral issues. Ethical solutions must be æsthetic as well as practical and humane. Life and art must mesh.

André Gide's *Journal* reveals just how much he made sense of his life through his art. Writing was his means of valorizing life. He was an obsessive writer, that's clear. He had to write it all down to make sense of it, in order to order it, to enlarge and enjoy it. Edouardo in *The Counterfeiters*, Gide's most accomplished creation of a writer character, calls his notebook his pocket-mirror: 'I cannot feel that anything that happens to me has any real existence until I see it reflected here.' (C, 142) A classic Gidean concept. At this level it is nearly impossible to separate art and life. And writing is thus vital to the Gide-writer's existence. Unless it's written down, he doesn't feel fully alive.

Joy should be the aim of life, and of art. André Gide is like D.H. Lawrence, Henry Miller and Joseph Campbell in this respect. Campbell called it 'following your bliss': 'if you are following your bliss, you are enjoying that refreshment, that life within you, all the time' (1988, 121). Campbell said in *The Power of Myth* that the artist is someone who follows their bliss: 'Poets are simply those who have made a profession and a lifestyle of being in touch with their bliss' (118). For D.H. Lawrence the business was simply a matter of being alive – really, fully and truly alive: 'To be alive, to be man alive, to be the whole man, that is the point',[1] Lorenzo asserted. Jacques Lacan called it *jouissance*. 'To make love... is poetry', Lacan wrote (143).

Life should be blissful, and art should help promote this rapture. To get *jouissance* you might have to be ruthless: 'Reduce everything to the ESSENTIAL', said André Walter in his *Black* notebook (AW, 77). He was talking about his novel, but for Gide that meant the whole of life. D.H. Lawrence spoke of the novel as the 'big book of life',[2] and Gide felt the same about writing in general.

André Gide's philosophies merge into one: spontaneity into freedom, renunciation into ecstasy. So do his artforms. The novel, the *récit*, the *sotie*, the lyrical pieces, all merge into the *Journal*. You can swap parts of *The Counterfeiters* or *Fruits of the Earth* with the *Journal* and not notice the difference. Gide's fiction, like that of John Cowper Powys and Henry Miller, is one with his diaries. The boundaries between fiction and reality are deliberately blurred. The fiction is a journal, while life is rigorously fictionalized in the *Journal*. Robert Graves spoke of his poetry as a 'spiritual autobiography'.[3] The *Bible* is regarded now by some as a great novel. Everything can become poeticized and personalized. If the *Bible* is poetry (some of it is), so ethics, æsthetics, philosophy, religion, art, history and literature all merge together in the modern, European mind.

Nothing new about this – this is a typical stance in the 21st century. In André Gide's work, though, it is more subtle than in most artists' work.

André Gide keeps his distance in numerous ways. He uses many literary devices. He plays with the reader. *L'Immoraliste* consists of the transcription of a story told to a friend; *The Pastoral Symphony* is a series of entries in a journal in two notebooks; *The Counterfeiters* is made up of multiple viewpoints complexly choreographed by a writer's journal; *Fruits of the Earth* features diary-style entries, poems, anecdotes, maxims, and a variety of voices. Thus, there are multiple layers at work; we can move from the text through narrators and stories told second-hand, to the author and the masks he wears.

André Gide loves to play, to change personæ, to wear masks, to transform his identity. A personality isn't fixed in Gide's work. There is no single voice in his books, as there is in, say, the works of Novalis or Thomas Hardy. Most writers have a recognisable voice, but not Gide. He changes. His ultimate style would be to have no style at all, to be pure prose, limpid and lucent.

Typically, André Gide's tone of voice is slightly formal, but relaxed, quite simple (he never goes for complex means of expression). Occasionally naïve, but usually well-informed. But there is a weariness, a desperation, a dissatisfaction under it which is expressed gently, but is nonetheless there.

Just as André Gide regarded *The Immoralist* and *Strait Is the Gate* as part of the same problem, so for him life, morals,

ANDRÉ GIDE

psychology, religion and sensuality are all one. They are all part of the same thing. The human individual unites them. The vehicle for this unity is the *Journal* – this is the interface of all these aspects of life. Gide's best creation is himself, his best work is his *Journal*. It is the same with Anaïs Nin. Her *Journals* were her finest creative work, but her most accomplished creation was herself, her own life.

Though short, André Gides books seem long and densely packed. How? He crams in a lot, for sure, but the real reason is that he naturally writes at a slow pace. He does not gush, like John Cowper Powys or Henry Miller (they both took pages and pages to say one or two things), or over-write and over-egg his stories, as Stephenie Meyer does (Meyer can't resist explaining every little thing). Gide is circumspect and contemplative. He wants the reader to stop and think (J2, 327). He wants a slow-motion kind of prose. His natural tendency is to proceed slowly, carefully, like a thoughtful pilgrim moving up some mountain to a Japanese shrine. Gide doesn't stop by the wayside and say, 'oh, look at this distracting object for a while.' He keeps walking, step by stone step, getting closer to his target.

We discern in the work of André Gide a fundamental tension that fuels all his art, all his life. It is, put barely, a tension between desire and detachment. This is it, the bare bones of the dialectic. Not between life and death, but between desire and restraint, between yearning for closeness and a longing for distance, between motion and stillness, between sex and boredom, between sinful sensualism and ascetic denial.

André Gide is eternally restless, and his art benefits from this. In 'The Roundelay of All My Desires' in *Les Nourritures Terrestres*, Gide writes:

> Entre le désir et l'ennui
> Notre inquietude balance
> (To, and fro, uneasily we sway,

ANDRÉ GIDE

between desire and listlessness [75])

Here André Gide swims, between desire and *ennui*. When he writes of art, which is very often, he is generally tempering his desires. He wants to give form to his experiences. Gide is an exact artist. He is not an Expressionist, not a hurricane like Michelangelo Buonarroti or Emil Nolde. His lyricism is a little like Claude Lorrain or Jean Baptiste Camille Corot among painters, gentle, restrained, wistful, with a little of the mannered, cultured Classicism/ Neo-Classicism of Jacques Louis David and J.A.D. Ingres mixed in.

André Gide writes quickly, after long bouts of thinking, of preparation (Pre, 306-7). To let everything sink in, the novel should be read slowly (J, 512). Gide veers from spontaneity in his writing – 'Of all my books there is none more spontaneous, more sincere than my *Nourritures*' (J, 521) – to a circumspect contemplation of each sentence. He speaks often of sentences, of making just the right kind of structure, which should be hidden from the reader (J, 182).

André Gide desired an effortless kind of writing, in which all the effort gone into creating it is hidden, which reads simply and elegantly. The reader must 'sink at every step into a rich soil', Gide commented (J2, 327). The reader must think, must ponder.

In his quest for a clear, elegant style, André Gide tried to get rid of all rhetoric, trickery, conceit and pomposity. Like his friend Paul Valéry, Gide hated ornamentation – anything that gets in the way (Pre, 318).

André Gide can write extravagantly (in Alissa's diary in *La Porte Etroite*, for instance, which he wrote easily and rapturously [Pre, 320]). But his natural inclination is to strip everything away. His settings, narratives, characters, philosophies and ethics are all products of this stripping away.

Gustave Flaubert dreamt of 'a book about nothing' (M. Allott,

ANDRÉ GIDE

242). It is a dream that has equivalences in abstract art: in Kasimir Malevich and Robert Ryman with their white-on-white square canvases, or the voids of Yves Klein, for example.

André Gide hated artists who tried to explain their work (Pre, 223). It should all be there. He imagined a preface for his fiction which would set forth two kinds of 'fictional objectivity': the first sees people and acts from the outside; the second, which is clearly Gide's preferred kind of art, is subjective, emotional and experiential. For this kind of writer, 'All the heaven and hell of his characters is in him' (J2, 392).

This inner space fiction aims to be realized as pure form. André Gide strived, like the Romanian artist Constantin Brancusi in his sculptures, for 'pure form'. A Neoplatonic ideal, perhaps, but an essential ingredient in the French artist's credo. One thinks of painters such as Piero della Francesca and poets such as Francesco Petrarch, and before them the Ancient Greeks, who sought pure form more passionately than most artists.

André Gide aligns himself with such humanist seekers of the essence. He is a classicist, a Renaissance artist, not a Romantic (Pre, 199).

Style is, as Marcel Proust noted, a question 'not of technique but of vision' (H. Block, 79). One must have 'a kind of focus', said Leo Tolstoy (M. Allott, 235). Gide's fiction is supremely focussed.

André Gide's searches for pure form produced many different kinds of fiction. The loose free-flowing notebook and part-poetry form of *Les Nourritures Terrestres* seems well-suited to its subject matter. The two – subject and form – are inseparable in modern art from J.M.W. Turner and Paul Verlaine onwards, but Gide did not always conceive the two together. His subjects seem to come first, and he dreams of putting them into prose for years. Books gestate in Gide's mind for decades sometimes.

The Immoralist seems just right, but the form of *Strait Is the Gate* is more problematic. The journal form André Gide feels very comfortable with, but it is tacked on the end of *Strait Is the Gate*. Such an important document should have been noted many times earlier in the text. Gide sacrifices many narrative possibilities in favour of religious fervour. In a note of 1908 he said:

> Sublime style – direct emanation from the heart; it is only through piety that it can be achieved, (J, 133)

André Gide means artistic as well as Christian piety. Purity through piety. Clear philosophies that stem from clear writings that in turn stem from a clear mind. Art and life; each one feeds the other in Gide's work.

Stendhal is André Gide's ideal of the clear-headed, clear-handed artist (who also happens to be French). When in doubt, Gide re-reads Stendhal's books to sharpen up his mind and pen (J, 188). The example of Stendhal reminds him that clarity is prime. Don't write unless you've got something to say, and then you must say it clearly, simply and truthfully (M. Allott, 128, 312). Too few artists adhere to this rule. It is the optimum state – only writing what you feel compelled to write. The rest is garbage. Thus Gide in 1930 wrote:

> I always take great joy in suppressing everything useless. My waste-baskets fill up with 'changes' that would have seemed mere stuffing; but what good is that false wealth to me? (J, 465)

The 'false wealth' is junk, trivia, banality. Unfortunately, television, magazines, radio, the internet, movies and all the media today are full of it. Your trash can is your best friend. When in doubt, throw it out.

Unfortunately, André Gide did not apply this editing process to his *Journal*. It is far too long – even in the edited-down version published by Penguin (that is, it is too long as a published book, as a book meant for the general public read to read). Anaïs Nin's

Journal, though longer, is much more dense and often more interesting (certainly more sensational – especially the diaries published after Nin's death, which detail her incestuous relationship with her father). In his fiction, however, Gide abided by his rule: 'do not linger' (Pre, 323). So he didn't.

André Gide has many good things to say about the art of writing. You could make a fascinating anthology of his sayings. Much of Gide's fiction is concerned with writing and the eternal question, *why write?* The reasons are manifold, he says: 'and the most important ones… are the most secret' (J2, 306). He writes to leave something after his death. So he evades fads and fashions. He aches for a timelessness in writing. Jean-Paul Sartre acknowledged the necessity of sharing things with other people (H. Block, 171).

André Gide writes to teach, to inform, to inquire, to help. There is a deep pedagogical motive behind much of Gide's fiction. 'Nathaniel, I will teach you fervour', says Gide's narrator, as if anybody can be 'taught' fervour. 'Nathaniel, I want to bring you to life', he says, at his most messianic. And he tries to do so (P, 36). 'Nathaniel, I will teach you that there is nothing that is not divinely natural', he cries (93), and the message hits home.

André Gide is a good teacher at times: he is distanced, but empathic; he is clear but very sophisticated; he knows when to let the neophyte fly free.

Through Michel in *L'Immoraliste*, Gide tries to teach, as Ménalque teaches Michel in the book. Alissa teaches Jerome in *Strait Is the Gate*. Gertrude teaches the minister in *La Symphonie Pastorale*. Lafcadio teaches Julius in *Les Caves du Vatican*. And Edouardo in *The Counterfeiters* teaches Bernard, Olivier, Laura, etc. The teaching is that life is of prime importance – life above art, above other forms of culture (or it is the other way around?). Freedom is the goal.

ANDRÉ GIDE

What is more glorious than a soul when it liberates itself? (J, 287)

The Counterfeiters (*Les Faux-Monnayeurs*, 1926) is the major work by André Gide that explores the nature of writing and the role of the writer. Imagination is greater than reality, yet Edouardo cannot 'invent anything' (C, 105). He merely observes people. Gide spoke of having someone to 'sit' for him, as a model poses for a painter, in *If It Die* (229).

Through this structure of novelists-within-novelists and novels-within-novels in *The Counterfeiters*, André Gide explored the rivalry between the 'real world and the representation of it which we make to ourselves' (C, 183). Image, meaning, text, representation – no wonder Gide is popular with post-structuralists, semioticians, postmodernists, and other cultural theory critics. He is an ideal subject for a study of the relation between reality, art and the artist.

Like André Gide, Edouardo in *The Counterfeiters* is a firm adherent of artistic purity. He is ultimately only a cipher for Gide's on-going explorations. This book is full of puppets in varying states of undress ('ideas, I must confess, interest me more than men', confesses Edouardo [170]).

The Counterfeiters is partly about the death of the novel, the demise of fiction. Coming hard on the heels of those two last great novels, *Ulysses* and *Remembrance of Things Past* (novels that can be seen as the Last Novels), *The Counterfeiters* destroys the delicate, fabric of fiction, the elegant web of postponed belief upon which fiction is founded. *The Counterfeiters* looks forward to the ready-made sculptures of Marcel Duchamp, the passionate subjectivity of American Abstract Expressionism and the highly intellectual, reflexive cinema of Jean-Luc Godard and the French New Wave.

Les Faux-Monnayeurs is a Pop Art novel, thirty years before the movement began, complete with xeroxes of the artist in several poses pasted into the work itself in the manner of Andy

ANDRÉ GIDE

Warhol. In *The Counterfeiters*, André Gide dons his coat of many coloured fictions and leads the critics a merry dance. This is a book in which 'the history of the book will have interested me (Edouardo) more than the book itself' (C, 170). So Gide brought out a *Journal of the Counterfeiters*, which he said he'd never do (despising, as we said earlier, artists' explanations). However, the book about the book is not better than the book itself. A central, heavily ironic conversation occurs between Olivier and Bernard:

> "...I don't know whether I shall write. If sometimes seems to me that writing prevents one from living, and that one can express oneself better by acts than by words.
> "Works of art are acts that endure," ventured Olivier timidly; but Bernard was not listening.
> "That's what I admire most of all in Rimbaud – to have preferred life."
> "He made a mess of his own." (C, 240)

This is one of André Gide's examinations of the relation of art and life, and which is more valuable. Arthur Rimbaud's life is the great illustration here: the greatest modern, French poet, who gave up writing aged nineteen to pursue 'life', what 'living' is, or was. The problem for us is that we don't have Rimbaud's life, only his poetry, which is tremendous. Rimbaud's life, like William Shakespeare's, or Plato's or Chuang-tzu's, is largely a mystery. Bits of paper, words, memories, a tombstone, changed landscapes – this is all that's left. The artist disappears (after decades, there's nobody left alive who knew Rimbaud personally).

But André Gide was interested in the role of the artist, as much as in the works themselves. His concern is the ethical conduct of the artist. What does the artist do, what is her/ his relation with her/ his art?, with society?, and with other artists? Perhaps Gide should have studied the original artist, the prehistoric shaman, the miracle-worker, the dancing sorcerer. The shaman is the ancestor of all artists, poets, priests, religionists, gurus, actors, etc. He might have gained a new insight into teaching, and what should be taught (however, Gide was also someone who seemed like he knew everything, and you couldn't teach him anything new).

André Gide was interested in refinement, in ontological transcendence. *The Notebooks of André Walter* (1891) reveals Gide aching for transcendence in at once adolescent pseudo-religious terms and in a mature, sophisticated way: 'Therefore, simple lines, schematic arrangement. Reduce everything to the ESSENTIAL.' (AW, 77) André Walter desires to make his writing tight, hard, gleaming as ice. But his gushes of feeling always smash his attempts at form: 'emotional ways made the sentence explode' (55). For this budding new author 'the sight of white paper intoxicates' (56).

In *Paludes* (*Marshlands/ Morasses*, 1895), the intoxication and the desire has gone. Satisfaction, the dam that holds back desire and keeps it alive, has broken. Desire has flooded the landscape to create marshlands. The young author is striving to write of nothing: nothing happens and his character is a nonentity: 'What I want to express is the emotion my life has given me: the boredom, the emptiness, the monotony' (P, 20). This mocking satire, with its *mise-en-scène* of monotonous greyness, 1890s bohemia and intense lassitude, ends with a 'List of The Most Remarkable Phrases in *Paludes*' (95). The narrator leaves a space for the reader to add to this list. Later, Lawrence Durrell has the character Pursewarden place an asterisk in a novel which refers the reader to a blank page. Durrell does the same in the book itself, *The Alexandria Quartet*. Both Gide and Durrell want the reader to do some work, to be active. Part of Gide desires a more active participation in art, an art integrated (like music) into the rituals of everyday life. Thus Michel in *The Immoralist* despises people who cannot recognize beauty until it has been transcribed and interpreted. The Arabs have this admirable quality, that they live their art, sing it, dissipate it from day to day. (I, 148)

Lafcadio (in *The Vatican Cellars*) is similarly impatient. He wants life head-on, with no mediation in between him and life. He hates 'all the scratchings out and touchings up' in writing (VC, 72). In life you just get on with it. With what? With 'living'.

A living art is a dream of many artists. André Gide moved towards the plastic arts, such as sculpture (loving, like D.H. Lawrence, the sense of touch), and the performing arts, such as music and theatre. Here the artist is the art, is one with the art. Presence is primary. Literature never has (or seems to have) the same presence as music or drama. Cinema is simulated presence – the screen is a barrier mediating the art. In literature, the word gets in the way. At least in music you deal with the business right in front of you. Music was ever important in Gide's life. Playing the piano made Gide more rapturous more often than writing did (you can see him playing piano in *Avec André Gide*).

CHAPTER FOUR

FERVOUR AND DESPAIR

THE IMMORALIST/ L'IMMORALISTE

O toi que j'aime, enfant! je te veux entraîner – dans ma fuite. D'une main prompte saisis le rayon; voici l'astre! Déleste-toi. Ne laisse plus le poids du plus léger passé t'asservir.
(O boy whom I love; I will carry you with me in my flight. Seize the sunbeam with an agile hand; behold the day-star! Away with your ballast! Let not the weight of the lightest part be a drag upon your freedom.)

André Gide, *Fruits of the Earth* (145)

The Immoralist (*L'Immoraliste,* 1902) crystallizes the fervour of *Fruits of the Earth*. It is a complex and dense book. It feels long, although it is a slim volume. André Gide does in a hundred and fifty pages what it takes other novelists hundreds more pages to do.

Michel, the central character, has summoned three friends to hear the story of the breakdown of his marriage, from the wedding in the 'little country church' in Northern France (I, 13), to the death of Michel's wife Marceline in North Africa. This is a descent into evil, into pain, into suffering. The last third of the book is a constant decline – and while Marceline degenerates, Michel becomes ever more alive.

Classically, André Gide begins his tale with the anti-hero's father's death (instantly adding a welter of œdipal associations and an evocation of the Law of the Father). The lovers are betrothed at Michel's 'dying father's bedside' (14). Michel is a scholar, a student and teacher of history. He treasures fine sentiments (15). He is an archetypal bourgeois character. He is of delicate health, and the first part of the book describes his decline into illness as he and Marceline travel down to North Africa.

The Immoralist is full of journeys, spiritual ones mainly, which are expressed as outward, restless movement. The couple go to Paris, then Marseilles and Tunis.

Michel begins to wake up, not to the ruins he visits in the Magreb, but to new sensations ('at the touch of new sensations, certain portions of me awoke' [19]). Michel is a product of a barren, patriarchal, Northern European world. It is seemingly inevitable that a new continent is going to wake him up. He is, after all, a sensitive soul – sensitive to what he's interested in. He continually acts selfishly, and ignores his wife.

Michel becomes ill. The couple go to Biskra, ever a favourite town for André Gide. Death touches Michel, but he finds they are staying in a beautiful place: he can see roofs then palm trees then the desert (25). Michel begins to fight to be alive. He is still weak, however. He does nothing, and even reading exhausts him. 'Existence is occupation enough', as he puts it (26). Which it is for many people.

André Gide is such a quick mover in writing. Other (lesser) writers might have spent chapters on Michel's decaying state (think of D.H. Lawrence or Marcel Proust). But Gide doesn't hang about. Straight away he introduces the major theme of homosexuality. Marceline brings in a young Arab boy. Michel notices at once that underneath his burnous he is naked (26).

Michel becomes fascinated with the boy Bachir and his healthy living in the present ('I had fallen in love with – his health' [28]). The will to live resurges in Michel: 'I want to live! I *will* live!' he thinks (29). He starts to concentrate on his body. It becomes a battleground for him, the site of life fighting death. His hyper-sensitivity creates delights now as well as pains. The André Gide of *Fruits of the Earth* is revisited here as Michel has fervent experiences. Rapture becomes the norm for a while:

> It was with rapture I passed into its [the garden's] shade. The air was luminous... I was excited – dazzled – rather than tired. I looked. The shadows were transparent and mobile... Light! Oh, light... every sound amused me... My touch was a caress; it gave me rapture. I remember... Was that the morning that was at last to give me birth? (pp. 38-39)

This is the language and fervour of *Fruits of the Earth*, but tempered by despair and lassitude. This is an older André Gide at work here. The 1902 book describes a rebirth nevertheless, ever a major theme. Michel becomes interested in lower, 'primitive' levels of civilization. He starts to move towards a free, spontaneous, sensual and detached, Gidean ethic. The ideological awakening in *The Immoralist* is mirrored on the physical plane by Michel's joy, and in his erotic yearning for Arab boys. At one point, he sees an image of Pan the Goat-god: a half-naked shepherd, complete with a flute (41). It's another rapturous moment when Michel's senses are coming back to life: 'it was a place full of light and shade; tranquil; it seemed beyond the touch of time; full of silence; full of rustlings...' (I, 41).

L'Immoraliste is a deeply psychological novel, and we buy it all readily. We don't see Marceline's point of view at all (or only mediated through Michel). It must strike her as odd that her new husband, the shy, studious and oh so sensitive, middle-class man should start hanging about with Arab youths, right in front of her. It must have been odd for André Gide's wife, one of the models for Marceline. A strange honeymoon.

The 1902 book is full of tensions: between heterosexuality and homosexuality; between domesticity and the open road; between conformism and freedom; between life and death; between Christianity and an Existential, modern form of paganism; between loyalty and rebellion; between selfishness and altruism; between the bourgeois and the sub proletariat – all these tensions are subtly and delicately and very skilfully teased out by André Gide. Michel embodies them all, he is the battleground (and the focus of the novel). His very being is at stake, but at what cost? His wife dies: the price is exceptionally high. The Nietzschean doctrine of the survival of the strongest has many casualties.

It is André Gide's triumph that he presents all of this without being judgemental. He acknowledges the positive aspects of bourgeois marriage and domesticity, while also realizing the necessity for freedom. Men want it both ways.

The African section of *The Immoralist* concludes with Michel acknowledging Moktir's petty crime of stealing some scissors. The Freudian symbolism of the scissors is subordinated here to Michel's sense of identification with the peasant values and homoerotic appeal of Moktir, something Ménalque picks up on later... (Michel describes watching Moktir with fascination in the mirror as he reads a book: 'there was something strange, I thought, in the brilliant and sombre expression of his eyes. Some kind of inexplicable curiosity made me watch his movements' [I, 44-45]).

So husband and wife go North, to Italy. On the last night, Michel feels himself burning with a kind of happy fever – the fever of life itself (47). North Africa and all it stands for –

ANDRÉ GIDE

homoeroticism, the peasant class, hidden violence, exoticism – has stained him. It carries over into Normandy, just as it did for André Gide when, in Northern France, he yearned for North Africa (the film director Pier Paolo Pasolini has many affinities with Gide in this respect – the same fascination of the highly educated, European, intellectual writer/ poet for the under-classes and homoeroticism of North Africa, the lure of the exotic, the rejection of Western/ European culture in favour of 'Third World' culture).

The Immoralist's Michel is very much a rebel in the modern, European, Existentialist tradition. He is on a vision quest – for authentic life. Friedrich Nietzsche features powerfully in André Gide's philosophy. He yearns for a deeper, more authentic kind of life, as did T.E. Lawrence, André Malraux, Henry Miller, Ernest Hemingway and D.H. Lawrence. Gide's way is gentler than those people, but no less radical.

Whether good or evil, Michel feels he must follow his desire in *The Immoralist*. To frustrate his desire is to frustrate his life. After a bout of violence, Michel makes love to Marceline. She becomes pregnant. They return to Paris and become involved in the social round of dinner parties and drawing-room evenings. Michel hates this shallow life. The past holds no magic for him now (50). It is the feeling of being in the present that has swept away the past (49).

Life in Italy had become richer and he became more selfish in his enjoyment (52). At Ravello, Michel feels rapture again: 'a delicious burning enveloped me, my whole being surged up into my skin' (55; this might be a line from André Gide's *Journal*). Heat and the sun are the vehicles for Gidean ecstasy (as well as expressions of it). Life opens out in the Mediterranean lands in *The Immoralist*: it is the same with Albert Camus, Norman Douglas, Lawrence Durrell, Anaïs Nin and others. They need the sun and heat.

ANDRÉ GIDE

Michel and Marceline share a single night of total joy when they make love – it is the highpoint of their relationship, described in rapturous terms by André Gide in L'Immoraliste:

> that first night of ours was our only one, the expectation and the surprise of love added so much deliciousness to its pleasures – so sufficient is a single night for the expression of the greatest love, and so obstinately does my memory recall that night alone. It was a flashing moment that caught and mingled our souls in its laughter... (62)

Michel hides his new self (58) while he says 'every day my life grew richer and fuller as I advanced towards a riper, more religious happiness' (59). The problem is: what to do with this new birth? You have to do something. What? Where? In Normandy, he seeks the external manifestation of his new inner strength. But the rainy, domesticated North of Europe cannot provide the nourishment he needs (as with Arthur Rimbaud). He starts to get interested in the farm workers. They are sub-proletariat, corresponding socially to the Arab boys. They are just as shy and twisted. But this is not what Michel now wants.

Michel starts to order his life: it begins to have a new pattern. He goes back to his studies, but his passion doesn't last long – nothing does in André Gide's fictional world. Michel projects his desires onto Charles and also gives Marceline some attention. He is still on his vision quest, though: 'What did I mean by 'living'? That is exactly what I wanted to find out' (88). This is the theme of the 1902 book.

The scene in The Immoralist with Charles in the pond is typical of this era: there are similar scenes of latent homosexuality in the fiction of E.M. Forster and D.H. Lawrence (from the same era – in Women In Love and A Room With a View, for instance). Bathing remains among the standard settings for expressions of homoerotic desire.

ANDRÉ GIDE

In Paris, Ménalque appears, still the itinerant teacher and pederast (and still very Wildean) of the *Fruits of the Earth* days. His conversation with Michel crystallizes the latter's desires. Ménalque presides over the intellectual side of Michel in *The Immoralist*. He is there to rationalize the irrational. So he appears at Michel's lecture on the Spenglerian/ Darwinian organic lives of cultures. Ménalque's way into Michel's being is through the intellect. It is right that Marceline, the emotional side of Michel, should dislike Ménalque.

Ménalque comes out with some very Wildean sayings:

> "One must allow other people to be right... it consoles them for not being anything else." (91)

This is typical of Oscar Wilde: the maxim turned into an icy put-down; self-righteous, self-conscious, witty, intellectual. Ménalque teaches Michel, just as he taught Nathaniel (as Menalcas) in *Les Nourritures Terrestres*, to get rid of possessions, to live spontaneously, to disregard memories. The speech Ménalque gives is pure André Gide, straight from *Fruits of the Earth*. But in amongst these ecstatic conversations the viper of dualism lurks: for that very night, after Michel's guru has gone, he finds out his wife has had a miscarriage. Real flesh-and-blood new life, the child, has died, while the life of the spirit, of the open road, which Ménalque represents, is being born. Michel has already chosen which of the two he wants.

Back to the farm he goes. This chapter in *The Immoralist* – chapter three of Part Two – is brilliant. André Gide moves along so swiftly (look at how much psychological ground Gide covers in such a short space). Michel gets involved with the farm workers; homosexual feelings return; Charles disappoints; Michel goes out poaching his own animals; he is fascinated by the incestuous exploits of a nearby family; there is a crisis when Charles discovers Michel has been poaching; he decides to sell the farm;

and he opts to go away.

From Paris the couple go to Switzerland. Marceline is becoming weaker. André Gide describes the Swiss interlude succinctly and poetically (139). Michel lives in an 'unspeakable ennui' (140). They descend through Italy, but it is windy and cold and very disappointing. The second honeymoon is a disaster. In the first, Michel nearly died, in the second, his wife does die. She is aware of what is going on. In a poignant moment she tells him:

> "I understand, I quite understand your doctrine – for now it has become a doctrine. A fine one perhaps… but it does away with the weak." (141)

Marceline is now one of the weak, yet she nursed Michel when he was weak, playing the surrogate mother.

Michel's doctrine is riddled with hypocrisy. The Darwinian/Nietzschean 'survival of the fittest' is fine if you're one of the fittest. If you're ill for a while, you go under; Michel has not learnt compassion. He remains an Existential outsider, unable in his masculine alienation to understand and care for another human being. The solidarity and sexuality he shares with the French farm workers or the Arab boys in the Magreb is shallow and short-lived. He has rejected what loves him. Ménalque said get rid of possessions and of course Michel regarded his wife as a possession. He got rid of her. He is a murderer, in a way, yet, like Albert Camus' *étranger* in *The Outsider*, he is indifferent to his crime. For him it is not a misdeed, it is the necessary outcome of his life's trajectory. He wouldn't do it differently if he had his life around again.

This is a very painful book, yet done with such a lightness of touch. It is André Gide's finest fictional work – in design and execution. *L'Immoraliste* is short but so dense, lucid and deep. It works well on the narrative, symbolic and ideological levels. There is no easy solution, nor an easy condemnation by the author/ narrator. Gide is equivocal, ambivalent. He sees every side, he sympathizes with every view.

The structural design is balanced in *The Immoralist*: the two journeys, the two stints on the farm, the conception and the miscarriage of the child (both baptized for Michel by blood). You could put a mirror in the book in the middle, in the Paris episodes, and see the two halves of the book reflecting each other seamlessly. So elegant is the design of *The Immoralist*, the pattern of the journeys and times of rest, the varied stages of birth and rebirth, the tension between movement and stasis. *The Immoralist* is a superb piece of literary architecture, a great example of design.

Few books are so seemingly slight and so densely packed as *The Immoralist*. André Gide said he composed the book in his head before writing it (J, 412). Certainly it has that sense of completeness about it, of all the elements being thought about and worked out in relation to each other before being committed to paper.

In the 1902 book, André Gide takes the theme of renunciation to extremes. The search for an authentic set of values continued throughout his life. Gide was careful not to become dogmatic. He remained ambivalent. In his *Journal* he expresses so many thoughts as negatives. He is a Buddhist and part-Gnostic, an advocate of the *via negativa* (the philosophy of mysticism which uses a 'negative' path to the divine).

On the question of influences, André Gide is firm. Johann Wolfgang von Goethe he admits is a major influence, but Goethe, like William Blake, Friedrich Nietzsche and Fyodor Dostoievsky only confirmed and clarified what he had already thought. Gide was concerned to be original, to be new. He also acknowledged that art must be useful. Reality must be tested, and so must art. 'The only thing that is worth anything in literature is what life teaches us', he remarked (J2, 420). But he kept his art nondidactic, and what *The Immoralist* teaches us is difficult to define. The message is that renunciation and rebellion have a high price, requiring a massive commitment. Michel is someone who 'follows his bliss', to use Joseph Campbell's term, but makes others suffer in the process (so, is it worth it? Or is it something that Michel must do, or that he would do anyway, despite the personal cost?).

This is the main criticism of *L'Immoraliste*: this blinkered, self-centred attitude of Michel's. Feminists could demolish the book, because of its chauvinism, its belief in physical and moral 'strength', its uncaring ending and ontological ambivalence. Michel treats Marceline abominably, but André Gide is aware of it. He offers a subjective reading of the events, seen not only from Michel's point of view, but also through the distorting processes of memory. Memory is an enemy in the book ('memory is an accursed invention' [I, 150]), and at key points in his story Michel is clearly over-compensating emotionally.

Memory plays a key role in *The Immoralist*, for the second honeymoon pivots around memory. Michel lives partly in the past (as do Jerome in *Strait Is the Gate*, and the narrators of *Fruits of the Earth* and *The Pastoral Symphony*). Michel tries to recapture heterosexual love in Sorrento and homosexual love in Biskra. But the boys are changed, they are older, uglier, and more squalid (sex is a means Michel employs of living in the present).

At this point the lustful, Nietzschean male could simply grab some younger, juicier boys, but Michel is becoming more and more alienated. His restless search for evil ends in weariness. At the very end of the 1902 book he says:

> "Take me away from here and give me some reason for living. I have none left. I have freed myself. That may be. But what does it signify? This objectless liberty is a burden to me." (157)

Michel's freedom in *The Immoralist* – freedom one supposes from bourgeois domesticity, from a Northern European life, from his former self and from all kinds of responsibilities – is non-creative. He can do nothing with it. It goes nowhere. It is 'objectless liberty'.

Similarly, when André Gide found out someone was going to do a thesis on the influence of Friedrich Nietzsche on his work, he wrote: 'It's flattering, but where can it lead?' (J2, 420). (No doubt there have been plenty of theses on Nietzsche and Gide, and Gide and many other philosophers, written since then). Gide throws himself into the future: how can life be improved? How can art improve life? What will the future be like? He and his art ask such questions. And Michel in *The Immoralist*, the academic historian who knows all about the past and how it affects the present, cannot predict the future, cannot make plans, has no idea what the future will be like. '"Lead me back"', he implores his friends. He is no Nietzschean Superman at this endpoint in the book; he has no will-to-power. He is will-less, directionless. He lives in a limbo, in the little house above the plain, doing nothing, having sex with his servant boy Ali. He is ready to be reborn again, because the story is really beginning.

André Gide can not see what would happen next perhaps because this important book was written at a similar point in his own life. He wrote *The Immoralist* partly to throw light on his own predicament (that is, to teach himself).

André Gide is not wholly satisfactory with endings to his books; neither was D.H. Lawrence. Their fictions were open. Gide took his story so far, then left it. The idea is perhaps now to throw away the book, as with *Fruits of the Earth*.

The Immoralist is the lyricism and fervour of *Fruits of the Earth* put into prose. The basic tenets are the same, except *The Immoralist* is fuelled by a new, more mature sense of despair. There is the same emphasis on the present and repudiation of the past. Michel likes Naples rather than Florence or Rome, for example, because Naples is alive and does not live half in the past (Gide did not like Rome when he first visited the Eternal City; similarly, Pier Paolo Pasolini enshrined Napoli and Calabria above Northern Italy). The past is a dead weight around the neck of the Gidean hero, like earthly possessions. 'Let go of everything', implores the Gidean self, 'let it all go and start to live.'

The All-Father in Naomi Mitchison's *Travel Light* advocates the same principle:4 to travel light. But it is the nature of this 'living' that André Gide (and few people) could define. He cannot go beyond a certain point: the intensity of the future is too much.

L'Immoraliste is a mid-life crisis novel, born of mature anxiety about the direction of one's life (André Gide was 33 when it was published). Michel cannot go any further; he needs to be led, like a dog (he compares his servant to a dog). He is an animal – worse, in some ways: de-civilized, with few of the values of bourgeois civilization left in him. He has no creativity, he cannot be a nomad, a peasant, a local. He is of course a classic, modern outsider, just like those of in the work of Knut Hamsun, Albert Camus, J.-K. Huysmans, and Jack Kerouac. The outsider's journey leads him (it's always a 'him' in modern, European literature) away from everything Western civilization holds dear – the family, home-life, education, Christian morals, etc.

The journey in *The Immoralist* is really a descent as well as a rebellion. Mersault kills the Arab, for no passionate reason, in Albert Camus' novel in *The Outsider*. André Gide too explored the implications of the motiveless crime, the actionless act. The pseudo-Buddhist resignation is somewhat pathetic. In *The Immoralist,* Michel, like Mersault, is indifferent to the after-effects of his act. For these outsiders it is no crime, merely an act, something that was unavoidable. Michel's life-trajectory is inevitable; it grows organically from his character. There is no saving him. It is not a tragedy, but a black comedy with irony upper-most.

Michel the Outsider cannot integrate socially anymore. He

can't relate to anybody, except on a casual sexual basis. The desert fruit of his self is indeed turned to ash.

We can see how far the novel as a literary form has come from, say, Thomas Hardy to André Gide. If Gide's *The Immoralist* were conceived as a Hardy tale, there would be more characters, for a start. Yet in Gide's novel there is the couple *alone*. There is no third party to intercede, to put the story in perspective. Michel has Ménalque, and Bocage, and Charles, and the Arab boys, but Marceline has no one. All Michel's friends are male – there is no female voice or presence to alter or soften his personality, his urge towards evil (the theme of the modern, European couple adrift in North Africa was revisited in *The Sheltering Sky* by Paul Bowles).

But Marceline is even more alone in *The Immoralist*. In Thomas Hardy's fiction there would be some other main characters to counterpoint the central couple. André Gide is very modern: he isolates his people. He strips away all novelistic baggage. He does away with extra characters, descriptions, foreign ideas. Hardy moved towards this type of fiction in *Jude the Obscure* (1895), but he never went as far as Gide.

André Gide's 1902 book, coming out only 7 years after Hardy's last novel (of 1895), is a huge development. The 19th century novel is transformed here into something more refined, more crystallized, more austere and ascetic. Gide's book has all the literary weight cut away from it. It is a slimmed-down novel, using only the basic material. Places, anecdotes, side-tracking, commentary, character, history, childhood, argument, humour – all of these traditional elements are cut out (or reduced to a bare minimum).

Yet this is a rich work, as rich as *Jude the Obscure*, though the rage is of a different order. This is a cool book. All of Gide's books are cool: he is an elegant writer, like Gustave Flaubert. The rage comes out of the implications and mechanics of the narrative, but not from the prose style, which doesn't rant and rave. *Fruits of the*

ANDRÉ GIDE

Earth is a book of passions, but it can be too flowery. *The Immoralist* damps down the fervour of *Fruits of the Earth*, focusses it, and mixes in despair and lassitude. It is Gide's most complete and satisfying work of fiction.

CHAPTER FIVE

RELIGION

...j'aime assez vivre pour prétendre vivre éveillé, et maintiens donc, au sein de mes richesses mêmes, ce sentiment d'état précaire par quoi j'exaspère, ou du moins j'exalte ma vie. Je ne peux pas dire que j'aime le danger, mais j'aime la vie hasardeuse et veux qu'elle exige de moi, à chaque instant, tout mon courage, tout mon bonheur et toute ma santé...
(I like life well enough to want to live awake, and so, in the midst of my riches, I maintain the sensation of a state of precariousness, by which means I aggravate, or at any rate intensify, my life. I will not say I like danger, but I like life to be hazardous, and I want it to demand at every moment the whole of my courage, my happiness, my health...)

André Gide, *The Immoralist* (95-96)

As with the other areas of André Gide's life, his concept of religion is full of contradictions. He moves from an austere, Bible-loving Protestantism of Northern Europe, through South European, more fervent Catholicism, to, finally, the open, sensual paganism/ pantheism of North Africa.

André Gide is forever torn between doubt and faith. In his

work, he is ironic, detached and critical, yet how much he yearns for pure belief. He is a humanist, and, as with Fyodor Dostoievsky, Friedrich Nietzsche and D.H. Lawrence, Gide exalts the figure of Christ. The Saviour embodies humanity in apotheosis. Christ is the highest that he can aspire to, Gide feels: he is the figure who has achieved the most refined kind of beingness. Gide admired Christ passionately. He was in awe of the altruism of Christ (naturally for someone so concerned with themselves). In Gide's art, as in the art of Thomas Hardy and D.H. Lawrence, the *Bible* is quoted many times. It is referred to in many ways, and is often quoted directly, and commented upon (Gide read the *Bible* regularly).

The titles of André Gide's books have Biblical connotations. The language of the *Bible* resonates inside the art of Gide, but for ethical and moral reasons, not for (as sometimes happens), the splendour of the prose or the imagery. It is the moral dilemmas the *Bible* raises that really interest Gide. Just as in life Gide travelled between Culverville in the Protestant North to Uzès in the Catholic South, so he veers from faith to disillusionment. He says he is neither Catholic nor Protestant, but 'simply a Christian' (J, 284).

'I am a creature of dialogue; everything in me is conflicting and contradictory', André Gide commented in *If It Die* (232). One can imagine him relishing arguments with mediæval theologians such as Thomas Aquinas or Francis Bacon if, say, time travel were possible.

André Gide is slippery. He recognizes the multiplicity of viewpoints in our modern, secular age. His religion is founded on a balance between the 'spiritual and the temporal, between soul and body. Each depends upon the other. There is no spirituality that transcends the body. The body is the vehicle, the expression, the manifestation of spirituality. André Gide does not, like Christianity, oppose soul and body. He acknowledges sensuality, as much as spirituality:

> I believe in the spiritual world and all the rest is nothing to me. But that spiritual world, I believe that it has existence only through us, in us; that it depends on us, on that rapport our body provides it. (*Journal*, 762)

André Gide adds that this is no mystical belief, but a statement of an observable fact. A human-centred religion for him. A faith that tries to ignore the body is valueless. The wonder and importance of Christ is precisely because he was a *human being*, because he lived *on Earth*, because he was subject to all the pains of the human condition. Christ went through human life, from birth to death and yet he was the Son of God, God Himself, on Earth. *There's* the mystery, the miracle of it all.

It's natural for poets to speak of Christ, not of St Paul, St Augustine, Quintus Septimius Florens Tertullian, Origen Adamantius or any of the many theologians that came along afterwards. André Gide, like any true artist, wanted to get to the heart of the mystery. He didn't want any veils getting between him and Christ. Gide regarded people such as John Calvin or St Paul as 'two equally harmful screens' between Christ and himself (J, 153). St Paul was indeed very damaging to Christianity in its delicate early stages (St Paul was paranoid, deluded, vindictive, obsessive, and certainly a person you *wouldn't* entrust with the task of spreading the word of a new religion).

In *The Pastoral Symphony* (*La Symphonie Pastorale*, 1919), André Gide shows how St Paul can poison a simple, Christian faith by bringing in that zealous doctrine of sin and death. Gertrude, at the end of her life, gets St Paul read to her. Christianity turns sour for her here: '"Sin revived and *I* died"', says Gertrude (PS, 69).

From St Paul onwards Christianity deteriorated. André Gide wanted pure religion, which is not possible, historically, in Christianity, as it was constructed out of at least thirteen belief-systems at its inception (as Weston La Barre demonstrated in *The Ghost Dance*). It was a thoroughly syncretic religion, and some aspects of the new Christian belief were heretical and also absurd for earlier faiths, such as Judaism (the idea of God being incarnated in a human being, for instance, or the notion of a messiah, or the concept of the crucifixion).

The problems are multiplied by the ensuing centuries, and numerous developments of Papal councils and decrees, internicence theological battles, and hundreds of theologians each adding their interpretation of texts written hundreds of years previously by people in very different circumstances.

André Gide's allegiance was not to any particular strand of Christianity whether Catholic, Anglican, Gnostic, Coptic, Methodist, etc), but the teachings of Christ. It is Christ himself whom Gide quotes most of all in his works. Christ becomes the measure of life on Earth, as far as humans are concerned. He is the model, the ideal life, the life lived as fully as Gide can imagine (except in the sexual sense, and there Gide's sensuality takes over). Christ is the ideal for self-conduct, for moral questions, for altruism, and for suffering.

Many of André Gide's characters identify with Christ – the spiritual Christ, rather than the historical Jesus – Bernard, Alissa, André Walter, Gertrude, even Michel in *The Immoralist* – they are moving towards a Christ-like state. God is the future, says Gide in his journals (J, 242), and God needs us: 'He depends on us. It is through us that God is achieved', an intriguing notion (J, 746).

Here is the balance between the spiritual and the temporal, between possession and renunciation (J, 434). For André Gide, the battleground is the soul. He identified this early on: 'Everything happens deep in the soul', said André Walter (AW, 22). Later, Gide became confused about this idea of the soul (J, 760).

It was for him an experiential reality, not a theory. Most of André Gide's fictions occur within the soul. 'Self' is the preferred term in contemporary literary criticism. In Gide's art, selfs search their souls, using literary devices: novels-within-novels, mirrors, journals, and characters-within-characters.

The Counterfeiters tackles religious questions, but relates them always to the self. Here the notions of self and world, poetry and reality, truth and falsehood, are called into question. Gide is not dogmatic; he will not side with any particular school of thought (though he sides with Edouardo, more than anyone else). Gide is a magpie, he will take from religion what he likes (reflecting the 'perennial philosophy' approach of the 20th century, of thinkers such as Aldous Huxley and Carl Jung).

When he sat in the St-Severin church in Paris on the Left Bank, André Gide enjoyed a sense of æsthetic contemplation that was not religious (J, 243-4). Gide could distance himself from religion. He could see it ironically, as if life itself were a game (J, 466).

Les Faux-Monnayeurs presents life as a game, one in which the artist is the best player. The artist doesn't win, s/he simply understands well the true nature of the game. Edouardo speaks of the necessity of depersonalization (C, 95), the negating of self that enables the artist to sink into her/ his subject.

In *The Counterfeiters*, André Gide plays all kinds of games. It is difficult to pin him or his narrator down. Also, of course, there is the realization that 'God is playing with us' (C, 222). No one is free; everyone's a puppet; not just the characters, but also the novelist. S/he is controlled by culture, the puppet-life is inescapable. It is all manipulation.

But this doesn't get the artist out of her/ his Existential quagmire; there is still the burning question: what to do with one's life, how to act? How to create? Robert complains in *The Counterfeiters* of the Symbolists that they were all style and no substance – they did not bring with them an ethical system (C, 127).

ANDRÉ GIDE

There is some truth in that view – the Symbolists certainly had style in abundance; Symbolism has to be one of the most highly refined artistic and literary movements in the history of Western culture. And very often it is the triumph of style over substance. But what style! Or was Symbolism a proto-postmodern movement, in which style *is* substance, in which surface is everything? (i.e., 'the medium is the message').

André Gide's art is the result of his search for an authentic ethical system, a system fully in tune with the multiple demands of modern life. Hence the emphasis on Christ: how useful is his example of what 'living' is? Very useful, Gide would conclude. The next problem is: how to incorporate it into one's life? In *Strait Is the Gate*, Gide describes the dangers of taking the religious life too far. He shows how Alissa's alienating doctrine, brought on by Jerome, culminates in a desire for holiness not happiness. Holiness is placed above happiness (SG, 87).

> 'What can the soul prefer to happiness?' I cried, impetuously. She whispered:
> 'Holiness...' so low that I divined rather than heard the word.
> My whole happiness spread its wings and flew away out of my heart and up to Heaven. (SG, 87)

But, both have their place, and a joyless sanctity is (rightly) condemned by Gide.

The search for authenticity is one of the hallmarks of André Gide's art. His characters search for their own kind of self-transcendence (to use theologian Bernard Lonergan's term),[5] they ache for Campbellian bliss, for Jungian individuation, for the beingness of Martin Heidegger. 'I never am; I am becoming', Gide wrote in a Nietzschean mood in *Pretexts* (Pre, 323).

His fiction is the record of people in the process of becoming. They have not reached the quiescence of Zen-like beingness yet. They are still struggling. They are on the journey. It is a process of stripping away the useless elements of the self. Michel in *The Immoralist* reduces his life to a bare minimum, as he struggles to understand his desire for evil. Gertrude in *La Symphonie Pastorale* struggles into being, becoming apotheosized in religious fervour (like Alissa in *Strait Is the Gate*).

In *The Notebooks of André Walter,* life can only be valorized for the yearning poet by the soul-union with his beloved. Later, the Gidean protagonist will desire a more diffuse kind of union. Lafcadio in *The Vatican Cellars* prizes 'above all things the free possession of his soul' (VC, 56). It's all a process of education, even if, as in *Isabelle*, that education leads to disillusionment.

Even disappointment is a useful thing to learn. The young human must learn to live with frustration say the psychoanalysts. The world is not as perfect as it was in the womb. Wishes are not granted, desires are not gratified instantly anymore. Pain becomes the great teacher. Realization is essential, even of the most basic, seemingly obvious things. 'I'm alive and that's magnificent', thinks the narrator of André Gide's *Prometheus Misbound* (P, 189).

Progress is essential, too. The progress is not towards self-knowledge (not to 'Know Thyself', as the commandment at the Temple of Delphi famously said), but towards self-realization. Not 'Know Thyself' but *Be Thyself*. Full beingness is the goal, a full-blooded, full-bodied sense of living. Gide shares this goal of beingness with poets such as Arthur Rimbaud, D.H. Lawrence, Rainer Maria Rilke, and Walt Whitman, and modern mystics such as Georg Gurdjieff (indeed, 'Be Thyself' might be a mantra that could be applied to numerous artists in the modern era).

For André Gide, the real drama was this struggle for authenticity (J, 481). It is a drama severely interiorized, played out within the individual. Gide's fiction is marked by a lack of social interaction. His tales are made up of small units that seldom interact with large social structures. His fiction does not always

ANDRÉ GIDE

deal with social pressures, like that of Thomas Hardy or Henry James. Gide's fiction tends to be thoroughly subjective, even in the social satires such as *The Vatican Cellars*.

The problems André Gide confronts all occur on the moral, religious and ethical plane. Few other characters are needed other than some suitably hyper-sensitive individual (super-sensitivity and acute self-consciousness are the prerequisites).

André Gide could easily produce tales based on people alone in marshlands. It is out in the desert that Gide wants to work – on himself and his art. In the wilderness the deepest debates rage, unchecked, and the individual's resolve is so much stronger. Or there is dissipation, and a descent into desuetude.

André Gide wants to go *beyond*: 'Go straight ahead. Pass beyond', he says in his diary (J, 437). Work through despair, he says; pain teaches. When you're finished with the book, throw it away. Art must give way to life. Art throws you out into life. Hopefully you should see things a little more clearly. Art should refresh.

Les Nourritures Terrestres is the major book of Gidean self-realization. The narrator proposes to teach the acolyte *everything*. Everything: sensations, restlessness, desire, places, love and most of all *fervour*. This is the opposite pole of André Gide's cool, critical, detached stance: *fervour*.

Fervour is religious, but it is the fervour of being alive, of waking up to life. It is non-doctrinal and pagan in its basic nature. André Gide's paganism, in which he sees Pan striding through the fields, is not opposed to Christianity; it melts into it. Pan and paganism, Christ and Christianity, the two merge.

In the art of André Gide, paganism and Christianity combine quite happily: the fusion had already occurred in the Neo-platonists and Gnostics of the early Xian era.

André Gide's Christianity is heavily Hellenized: it is shot through with the spirit of first century Alexandria. His paganism is tempered by an austere Catharism. Fervour burned into him at an early age (If, 176), and fuelled both his paganism and Christian feeling. Gide is in many ways a simple soul. His art is complex but he is often so simple.

In *Et Manet in Te* and *The Intimate Journal*, André Gide portrayed himself as a love-sick teenager, yearning in a gushing fashion for his beloved Madeleine: 'I cannot live without her love' (Et, 70).

Like Pan, André Gide steps through the world looking for sensuality. His paganism acknowledges many gods and many possibilities. At the same time, Gide yearns for Protestant religion as embodied in Christ, and in particular in the scriptural Christ of the *Gospels*.

André Gide's paganism contains aspects of Neoplatonism, Hellenism, pantheism, and atheism, as well as Sufism and fervent, icon-kissing Catholicism. The gospel of his paganism is *Fruits of the Earth*, but his pagan stance is also found in *The Notebooks of André Walter*, *Paludes*, *Urien's Voyage*, *Oedipus*, *Theseus*, *The Immoralist* and *Corydon*, among others.

There are similarities between his paganism and that of Oscar Wilde, Arthur Rimbaud, J.-K. Huysmans, Plato, the Taoist philosopher Chuang-tzu, Sankara and the Zen Buddhist mystic Hui-Neng. It is a paganism that seems to accommodate anything, but is in fact very austere and highly individual. It is founded upon a modernist exaltation of the individual.

It is the power and sanctity of the individual that André Gide loves in Classical Greek tragedy, which gets rid of unnecessary æsthetic baggage and presents people on their own, in an isolation which Gide aimed for. Gide loves purity; he is the artist of extremes (P, 86). Purity in Gide's *œuvre* means being pushed to extremes. It is an ontological as well as æsthetic stance. So typical it is of Gide to write in his "Thoughts on Greek Mythology": 'The first condition for understanding the Greek myth is to believe in it' (Pre, 228).

A Classicist among Romantics, André Gide loves the naturalness of Greek mythology, the Ancient Greek way of life which exalted the body, the individual and pleasure (among other things). In *L'Immoraliste* Michel begins to wake up to the kind of life Gide aimed for:

> Il y avail ici plus qu'une convalescence; il y avail une augmentation, une recrudescence de vie, l'afflux d'un sang plus riche et plus chaud qui devait toucher mes pensées, les toucher une à une, pénétrer tout, émouvoir, colorer les plus lointaines, délicates et secrètes fibres de mon être.
> (There was more here than a convalescence; there was an increase, a recrudescence of life, the influx of a richer, warmer blood which must of necessity affect my thoughts, touch them one by one, inform them all, stir and colour their most remote, delicate and secret fibres of my being. [52])

CHAPTER SIX

PHILOSOPHY

André Gide does not have a fixed, fully-worked-out and complex philosophy. If he does, it is in constant flux. A constant in Gide's whole life's work is *change*. Nothing is eternally fixed for him. Generally, his philosophy is one of self-refinement.

André Gide is a moral writer, a humanist who tackles the human condition head-on. His solutions are individual, creative, and non-dogmatic. You can only save yourself, says Gide. Teachers have a limited usefulness. His Christianity moves towards Gnosticism, and his ideas are Oriental in flavour. His Protestant-tinged philosophy has a strong sense of duty, loyalty and ethics. His ethics are æsthetic and transcendent: 'Morality is a function of æsthetics', he asserts.

In the *Preface* to *The Immoralist*, André Gide writes that the statement of a problem does not imply its solution. He lets the reader judge for themselves. Many writers cannot resist offering a voice-of-God judgement on some action of their characters (think of Thomas Hardy at the end of *Tess of the d'Urbervilles*, when he tries to play God and pass judgement upon Tess's fate).

Modern novels try not to do this. Anyway, says André Gide,

ANDRÉ GIDE

'in art there are no problems that are not sufficiently solved by the work of art itself' (I, 8). This recalls William Wordsworth's dictum (which Lawrence Durrell took up): that the work of art shall create the taste by which it is to be judged.

André Gide is multi-faceted as a writer and thinker. He is, like most novelists, all of his characters. He is both Edouardo and Bernard, Lafcadio and Julius, Alissa and Jerome. He remains deliberately distanced, while at the time identifying deeply with certain characters. *Fruits of the Earth, Strait Is the Gate, The Immoralist* – these are clearly deeply personal works, that mean much to Gide. In the more playful pieces, such as *The Vatican Cellars* or *The Counterfeiters*, Gide keeps more of a distance, and is careful to cover his tracks.

Albert Camus too keeps his distance in his fiction. He keeps inviting us to judge Meursault's murder in *The Outsider* throughout those protracted courtroom scenes, yet his narrator remains impartial. *L'Étranger* develops the impersonal stance of *Le Immoraliste,* and it's easy to see in Michel the forerunner of Meursault. Michel, at the end of *The Immoralist*, doesn't care much what he does. He leaves it up to his friends. Meursault is more detached, and more philosophical than Michel. His stance is more extreme. While Michel feels some anguish at his wife's death, Meursault thinks:

> one might fire, or not fire – and it would come to absolutely the same thing... To stay, or to make a move – it came to much the same. (*The Outsider*, 62)

Lawrence Durrell says a similar thing at the beginning of his novel *Nunquam*: 'Asleep or awake – what difference?'[6] It is Samuel Beckett who most fully explored this Existential stance which veers between stupidity and oblivion.

To not care what happens next, this bleak view (or happy death) seems particularly masculine. You do not find it so much in women writers. It is masculinist, rebellious, pseudo-philosophical, and uncaring. It doesn't take into account other people. It is affectionless, non-empathic and somewhat immature.

In the fiction of Albert Camus and André Gide, however, there is a tremendous sense of social responsibility, of commiment and action, something you don't see so much of in the fiction of Samuel Beckett or Lawrence Durrell. English writers shy away from political prophecy and action (but there are some notable exceptions), while French writers readily embrace public argument.

Despair is more public too in French fiction, it seems. Existentialism is so much a product of the French mind and culture (and German culture, of course). Despair is one of France's specialities (and a speciality, in a more raw form, of Scandinavia). Thus Gustave Flaubert wrote in *Madame Bovary*:

> She was not happy; she never had been happy… Life was one great lie! Every smile concealed a yawn of boredom… (275)

Yet the self-pitying of characters such as Werther (Johann Wolfgang von Goethe) or Emma Bovary (Gustave Flaubert) or Heathcliff (Emily Brontë) or Jude Fawley (Thomas Hardy) is not the way of André Gide's or Albert Camus' characters. Their aim is happiness. The whole of *Fruits of the Earth* is a plea for more happiness:

> Heureux pensais-je qui ne s'attache à rien sur la terre et promène une éternelle ferveur à travers les constantes mobilités.
> (Happy, thought I, the man who is attached to nothing on earth and who carries his fervour unremittingly with him through all the ceaseless mobility of life. [56])

It is a very naturalistic kind of happiness. No frills, no tricks, no extras, no preparation, no regret, just the basic happiness. Mersault in Albert Camus' *A Happy Death* defines happiness thus:

ANDRÉ GIDE

"Everything else that would happen to me would be like rain on a stone. The stone cools off and that's fine. Another day, the sun bakes it. I've always thought that's exactly what happiness would be." (31)

The early André Gide, of the *André Walter* days (early 1890s), was more fervent than the young Camus:

[The soul] should find happiness not in HAPPINESS but in the awareness of its violent activity... My life will be more intense, my soul more vigilant. (AW, 26)

André Gide wants to be awake and aware, like his Ménalque, who, in *The Inmoralist*, says he keeps his life precarious: he hates security, and has a 'horror of rest'; he hopes to intensify his life by keeping on the edge (I, 95). Later Gidean characters live on the edge, such as Armand in *The Counterfeiters*, who comments:

That dividing line between existence and non-existence is the one I keep trying to trace everywhere. (C, 255)

Pleasure remained one of André Gide's main goals to the end of his life, though it became increasingly bound up with politics.

Most of André Gide's philosophical solutions are based firmly on the individual. He is a master of detached presentation. He withholds glosses and commentary. These he saves for his *Journal*. The ending of *L'Immoraliste* is superbly controlled – an example of his ideological restraint.

The apotheosis of his disinterestedness is the 'gratuitous act', which André Gide defined in *Prometheus Misbound* thus:

Neither interest, passion, nor anything else. A disinterested act, self-born, an act without an end in view; and therefore without a master; a free act; an autochthonous Act! (P, 107)

The gratuitous act is for André Gide the ultimate statement of individuality. In it the individual is free – free of authority, free of society and its *mœurs*, free of the influence of other people, free to be oneself. Escape can then be complete. It is a product of 'the *negative unforeseen*' (ib., 68). It is an act of total responsibility (115); it aims to bypass all the mechanisms of society; it aims to defuse civilization – to go against, really, the universe itself.

The 'acte gratuit' is André Gide's method of undoing the laws of physics. It hopes to be the living manifestation of the Law of Indeterminacy. But Gide's gratuitous act is very human. It is not totally impersonal. It pivots on chance, yes, but that is a human perception. The gratuitous act is a human construct. It is the ultimate way-out, an escape clause for alienated men. It is a way of kicking things into action, of making things happen.

'"Nothing ever happens"', moans the narrator of *Paludes* (30). The hobos groan the same way in *Waiting For Godot*, that nothing ever happens. Nothing happening – it's the great beginning for a work of art. Start at the rock bottom and work on up.

Lafcadio in *The Vatican Cellars* (*Les Caves du Vatican*, 1914) embodies the gratuitous act. He is an ambiguous figure. André Gide tried to build him high as the ultimate free spirit. He has no family, no ties, no background, and no job, yet he is an aristocrat, erotic, with no politics – a rebel, a precursor of the Dadaists and the Beat generation, a future art terrorist. On the train from Rome he thinks: 'One imagines what would happen if...' (VC, 177). *Something* must happen. Things get so bleak in the fictional outsider's life that anything happening would be good. Anything at all.

The ultimate gratuitous act in *The Vatican Cellars* is the perfect murder, the motiveless crime, doing something not even for the sake of it, but just doing it. Here Buddhist *karma* is subverted (one life feeding into another), and the cosmic wheel of Hindu *samsara* is broken (the cycle or wheel of existence: Buddha said that *nirvana* and *samsara* were one – a very profound statement).

Or so Lafcadio hopes. He is the one who dares, who makes the leap between the imagined and the deed. He is the artist of life, a directionless shaman. OK, *do it*. He does it. He plays (in) the game.

Fleurissoire scratches him badly; he bleeds; but it's done it. It's not the act that fascinates him, however. He is supremely self-centred: 'It's not so much about events that I'm curious, as about myself' (VC, 185). Earlier he says he would love to meet himself: 'I think I should take a great fancy to myself' (178-9). Of course he would! As well as being an outsider and a rebel, he's also a supreme narcissist (as all bohemian, artistic outsiders have to be. Maybe all artists are, too). Narcissism is built-in to being an artist, perhaps. French philosopher Julia Kristeva thinks so: for her, creativity is related to death, fear, and the void: writers are among those most enmeshed in grappling with a fear of the void: '[t]he writer is a phobic who succeeds in metamorphizing in order to keep from being frightened to death; instead he comes to life again in signs', Kristeva noted in *Powers of Horror* (38).

Art, for Julia Kristeva in *Histoires d'Amour*, creates both the subject and the object, it is the 'possibility of fashioning narcissism and of subtilizing the ideal' (1984, 21). This certainly describes many of André Gide's protagonists, who become the chief object of their scrutiny. They are interested ultimately only in themselves.

For Julia Kristeva, the narcissistic impulse developed in Neoplatonism, out of Greek mythology: with Neoplatonism, a new kind of love is born, one founded on interiority and autoeroticism. Narcissus loves himself, he is both subject and object. His real object of desire is an image of himself – that is, representation, art. Kristeva writes in "Narcissus: The Insanity" in *Tales of Love*:

> He loves, he loves Himself – active and passive, subject and object…
> The object of Narcissus is psychic space; it is representation itself,

fantasy. But he does not know it, and he dies. If he knew it he would be an intellectual, a creator of speculative fictions, an artist, writer, psychologist, psychoanalyst. He would be Plotinus or Freud. (116)

Narcissus in Ovid's poem is in love with an image, a representation of the beloved (himself), much as the artist is. Although he kills himself for falling in love with a fake, Narcissus nevertheless goes about dealing with his idealism by fetishizing his own image. As Julia Kristeva remarks, 'instead of having to create what will enable him to equal his ideal – a work, or an idealized object to love – Narcissus will fabricate an ersatz' (ib., 126). This is what André Gide's protagonists do. They create the idealism from their projections. Poets are in love with their self-created images. They have to be: it's their 'truth'. Poets are 'fascinated by images on the one hand, in quest of truth on the other' (ib., 131). Artists recognize their love of images even as they adore them. The two things, representation and 'reality', constantly fuse in a way that still confuses observers.

The gratuitous act in André Gide's fiction is terrifying because of its selfish violence. Meursault kills the Arab in Albert Camus' story, but the long court case and philosophical discussion that follows his act softens the violence, and makes it all ridiculous. Lafcadio's murder in *The Vatican Cellars* is much more difficult to deal with.

The problems begin with Lafcadio's personality. Like the characters in *The Counterfeiters*, the people in *The Vatican Cellars* are thinly sketched. They are shallow, puppet-like, unbelievable. Though harsh and supercilious, Lafcadio doesn't seem capable of such a murder. It is a problem, partly, of language. He thinks of his act as a game, a chance event. It is, in fact, a murder.

The stakes are high – the highest possible, in truth, for a humanist such as André Gide, who values human life so highly. In *The Vatican Cellars*, Lafcadio plays with another person's life, like he might play chess. The idea is to avoid all the consequences of the act, like a child who, delighting in being 'naughty', knocks over a pot of paint. His total disregard for the consequences is a sure sign of immaturity. Lafcadio soon faces the results of his act, with some ironic touches from Gide. But the gratuitous act remains a philosophical idea not grounded in experience, and not very plausible.

Jerome in *Strait Is the Gate* is also very immature about things at times. He acts like a teenager in his love-affair with Alissa ('Work, efforts, pious acts, he offered them all up, mystically, to Alissa' [SG, 23]). Perhaps he exaggerates, as he is remembering from ten years ago. In this tale, André Gide undoes his credibility. With its palpitating, quivering lips, blushing cheeks, hot flushes, trembling eyes, clasped hands, embarrassed silences and collapses onto the knees, the whole retinue of clichéd gestures from the 19th century romantic novel, the Jerome-Alissa romance is a flabby affair that is not convincing. The moral here is, ultimately: wake up and *realize*, before it's too late.

CHAPTER SEVEN

SENSUALITY

> Certes jamais aucune gloire ne vous vaudra, adolescence de nos
> cœurs! Aspirant tout avec délices, en vain cherchions-nous à lasser
> nos désires; chacune de nos pensées était une ferveur...
> (Ah! no later glory will ever equal that adolescence of our hearts!
> Rapturously inhaling every breath that blows, we tried in vain to
> exhaust our desires; every thought was a fervour...)
>
> André Gide, *Fruits of the Earth* (59)

Water is one of André Gide's favourite symbols, as with writers like D.H. Lawrence and Anaïs Nin. The sensuality and symbolism surrounding Gide's use of water is of life and freshness: the quenching of thirsts. He does not use water in the same way that D.H. Lawrence does, as a vast repository of symbolism. Water in Gide's fiction appears as a cool drink (in *Fruits of the Earth* throughout, and in *Urien's Voyage* [42]). There are the stinking marshes of *Paludes*; the pond in *The Immoralist*; the rain and the storm in *The Notebooks of André Walter* (63); but most often Gide uses water in the form of the ocean. Not the seething Great Mother sea of rebirth, but the sea of travel, of voyages, of movement. Gide's sea is, of course, the Mediterranean, which connects him back in time to Ancient Greek civilization, and to Africa. The voyage from multicultural Marseilles to Arabic North Africa is his voyage. It's the one he went on most – if not physically, then certainly mentally, in so many daydreams:

> Départ de Marseille. Vent violent; air splendide. Tiédeur precoce; balancement des mâts. Mer glorieuse, empanachée. Vaisseau conspure par les flots. Impression dominance de gloire. Souvenir tous les departs passes.
> (Departure from Marseilles in a violent wind. A magnificent day. Unseasonably warm. Rocking of the masts. A glorious, white-crested sea and wave-whipped boat. A triumphant impression of glory. The recollection of all past departures.) (*Fruits of the Earth*, 109)

Sensuality in André Gide's fiction is often ecstatic. Bernard feels bursting with life in *The Counterfeiters* (C, 242), a typical moment of Gidean joy. In *If It Die*, Gide tells how he experienced 'the true lyric ecstasy' (If, 162). Sensualism in the art of Gide is not a philosophy, nor even a systemized way of being. It is something unplanned for, experienced spontaneously. It means concentrating on the present moment, as he explains in "Letters to Angele":

> Sensuality... consists simply in considering as an end and not as a means the present object and the present minute. (OC, 3, 220)

This is the ontological stance of *Les Nourritures Terrestres*, and also of much religious mysticism: the living in the here and *now*, without recourse to the past, or future, or even such complicated and complicating concepts as God or the sacred ('be fully present', the mystics say – not always so easy to achieve! As Gide put it in *Fruits of the Earth*: 'We only exist, Myrtil, in the *here* and now' (62).

ANDRÉ GIDE

André Gide preferred not to be called a mystic, despite the mystical nature of much of his art. But he is a poet, and his optimum mode of being, if it is not mystical, is certainly poetic. This is what Edouardo calls it in *Les Faux-Monnayeurs*: '[t]he only existence that anything (including myself) has for me, is poetical' (68). Another time he calls it 'lyrical' (C, 277).

Glory is internal in André Gide's works. If there is joy, it usually grows from within. This is only right for a deeply interiorized writer, someone who explores every facet of his being. The outside world is there, but it is the interior struggles that Gide is really interested in. Nature and its beauty is sometimes praised – most enthusiastically in *Fruits of the Earth*.

André Gide's favourite landscape is the desert. In the Sahara Desert is experienced the 'incredible, absolute silence', which Paul Bowles called 'the baptism of solitude' in *Their Heads Are Green*:

> Immediately when you arrive in the Sahara, for the first or the tenth time, you notice the stillness. An incredible, absolute silence prevails outside the towns… Then there is the sky, compared to which all other skies seem mere faint-hearted efforts. Solid and luminous, it is always the focal point of the landscape… You leave the gate of the fort of the town behind, pass the camels lying outside, go up into the dunes, or out onto the hard, stony plain and stand a while, alone. Presently, you will either shiver and hurry back inside the walls, or you will go on standing there and let something very peculiar happen to you, something that everyone who lives there has undergone, and which the French call *le baptieme de la solitude*.

In *Amyntas* (1906), André Gide wrote of the desert:

> The sky in the west was of a most pure blue, so transparent that it seemed still suffused with light. The silence became wonderful; one could not conceive even of a song there. I felt that I loved this land perhaps more than any other… (17)

ANDRÉ GIDE

The early fiction of André Gide is full of glories, of ecstatic sensualities. In *Strait Is the Gate,* there is a 'shimmering glory' of a sunset (102), but such pæans to nature are rarer in the later works. Even in *Fruits of the Earth* the ecstasies are more interiorized, more to do with states of being than with external nature.

But André Gide always tried to capture the essence of a landscape. In *Amyntas,* he returned to his hallowed town of Biskra in North Africa:

> What do I come to seek here again? – Perhaps, just as a body afire finds joy in diving naked into cold water, any spirit, stripped of everything, drenches in the ice-cold desert its fervour.
> The pebbles on the ground are beautiful. The salt gleams. Over death floats a dream.
> I took one of these pebbles in my hand; but no sooner was it off the ground than it lost its brilliance, its beauty. (112)

The natural world is glorified, but in a stylized way. André Gide admits he cannot describe the desert as it actually is:

> I should like to linger another day or two in this country; but even should I live here thirty years, I should find nothing to say about it… one cannot depict it as it is; one can only attempt to describe or talk about it. (A, 52)

But this is the place where André Gide was re-born, where he became truly alive, where he rebelled and threw off the ethics of his Northern European childhood, and where he found homosexual love.

In *Amyntas* he acknowledges that the desert kills art, that it is a 'hideous… intemperate' place. The answer, Gide says, is to resign oneself to the landscape itself:

> In the desert, one should content oneself with the education, the exaltation, I mean, which it offers, and know how to make one's dispositions accordingly. (A, 40)

ANDRÉ GIDE

André Gide talks about being uplifted by the 'warm luminous air' in *Les Nourritures Terrestres* (112), or dazzled by 'lovely light' (ib., 152), but he is always aware that his experiences must soon become poetry. He is like a painter who can't stop painting, or a photographer who has to snap away at nature before it becomes real to her/ him. Gide (via his narrator) experiences things, but always seems to be thinking ahead, musing on how to turn life into art.

In many ways, André Gide values art above life. Art is more beautiful to him than life. In art a purity can be attained that can never quite be grasped in life. It is this relation between art and life that Edouardo investigates in *The Counterfeiters*. It is the business of the novelist, Edouardo contends, to solve the problems life cannot solve (C, 281). Halfway through *The Counterfeiters*, Edouardo recognises the 'deep-lying subject' of his book: 'the rivalry between the real world and the representation of it which we make to ourselves' (C, 183).

What André Gide tries to do in his sensualisms in his art is to retain the childlike wonder of life and the world so necessary to the artist. Like a mystic, he wants to be in a perpetual state of wonder. In *Fruits of the Earth,* he writes:

> Dès ce jours, chaque instant de ma vie prit pour moi la saveur de nouveauté d'un absolument ineffable. Ainsi je vécus dans une presque perpetuelle stupéfaction passionée. J'arrivais très vite a l'ivresse et me plaisais à marcher dans une sorte d'étourdissement.
> (From that day onward every moment brought me its freshness as an ineffable gift, so that I lived in an almost perpetual state of passionate wonder. I became intoxicated with extreme rapidity and went about in a sort of daze.) (F, 28)

Elsewhere in *Les Nourritures Terrestres*, André Gide admits that his sense of wonder may have a mystical edge to it:

ANDRÉ GIDE

...you may call my amazement of this religious, if you like. I am amazed at everything on this earth. Let us call my stupefaction worship. (175)

André Gide is an intuitive artist: first he feels, then reflects: 'I feel that I am', he says (F, 173). This is undoubtedly true. But while he's feeling he's also writing. The two things are synonymous for him: art and life. Life would very impoverished without art, and art doesn't need life that much. There is an element in the art of Gide that yearns for the ultimate kind of purism in art: an art that has no relation to anything but itself.

This is Edouardo's dream in *Les Faux-Monnayeurs*: to strip the novel of everything unnecessary. Ideas interest Edouardo more than people he says (C, 170), and earlier he states: '"I should like to strip the novel of every element that does not specifically belong to the novel"' (C, 70). This is also Gustave Flaubert's dream, finding its great exponent in Samuel Beckett, whose fictions, like Gertrude Stein's poetry, are pure language, with barely any reference to the outside world.

André Gide doesn't achieve Beckettian purity, but comes close: particularly in *Paludes*, his most Beckettian work, which takes place in a grey swamp.

In all of André Gide's work there is a wonder at the world, and a joy in simple things such as the weather, water, and music. To these simple but deep pleasures he kept returning, in his art as well as in his life.

CHAPTER EIGHT

LOVE

> She is the only one I love in the world, and I really cannot love anyone but her... I have never wanted anything but *her* love, *her* approval, *her*... I have not ceased loving her... My entire work is inclined toward her.
>
> André Gide, *Intimate Journal* (in Et, 70, 75, 77)

Love in André Gide's art, whether heterosexual or homosexual, is restless, painful, searing, full of yearning and regret and mistaken perceptions. In the man-woman affairs, the woman is idealized and loved-from-a-distance, as with mediæval courtly love (it's the *amor lonh* – love from afar – of the French troubadours and the Italian *stil novisti*). She is mis-perceived by the lover. As in Thomas Hardy's fiction, in Gide's stories there is a gulf between the lover and his/ her beloved. The object is in flux, while the subject only admits constancy. The failure of Gide's characters' love-affairs stems from an inability to make a meaningful connection with the beloved. This is true of most love-tragedies. In Gide's fiction the failure is a personal one. It does not stem from societal forces, but from inner weaknesses.

Jerome in *Strait Is the Gate* (*La Porte Étroite,* 1909) is blind to Alissa's real needs. Michel in *The Immoralist* is oblivious to his wife Marceline. The men are selfish and immature; they are self-absorbed, too concerned with themselves to see anyone else fully. The women are loyal, caring and terribly mistreated. They are ignored. They are passionately desired, yet their own desires are not noted. *The Immoralist* and *Strait is the Gate*, both narrated by male characters remembering former deeds, feature two aspects of the typical Gidean, heterosexual relationships. *Strait Is the Gate* deals with a Victorian-style love-affair; it is a reworking of Thomas Hardy's *Jude the Obscure*, in some ways. The battleground is, as in *Jude the Obscure*, religion, and the ideas of sin, sexuality, soul, and immortality. God, faith and a monastic life are all discussed. Thomas Hardy is savage, while André Gide is gentle. There is much self-hatred in Hardy's 1895 novel, but both Alissa and Sue Bridehead burn with a fierce, Christian piety. It is interesting to note in both books the negative influence of men on women.

Much of *Strait Is the Gate* is stilted and strained; Alissa and Jerome act like fourteen year-old kids in puppy love. They are kids even at the end of the tale. Jerome ends up a quivering wreck, a spineless, wet, flabby, bourgeois scholar. He has no will, no energy, no life in him. Alissa sublimates her fire into pure faith, like Sue Bridehead did in *Jude the Obscure*. It is a case of mistaken projection. Identities are confused; perception is muddled; reality and the dream and switched.

André Gide's depictions of homosexual affairs are clearer: the (European bourgeois) character typically meets some younger (usually Middle Eastern) boy and they have sex. Gide described himself as a pederast (fond of young boys). Homosexual encounters in his books usually occur between older and younger men. The male love-object is not the equal of the protagonist, intellectually or socially, but is the superior physically (and sensually). The boys are a lower class, they are poor. Yet they dominate the relationships. They are closer to life, to the physical, sensual aspects of life. In short, they are more alive, and they show the older, Western men how to live.

There is in André Gide's fiction and in his European, intellectual, male protagonists a masochism, a gentle submission to the primitive sexuality embodied in these young, streetwise Arabs. Gide's European men are taken over. They are often impotent. Jerome shows a massive lack of will-power in *Strait Is the Gate*. He sees the door of Alissa's bedroom as a narrow gate that's difficult to enter. He can't push his way into heaven. The door works as a sexual barrier, standing in for Alissa's sex (with all the usual symbolism and prohibitions), but also as the eye of the needle in Jesus's parable in the *Gospels*. At the end of the story, Jerome slumps down outside Alissa's house. He can't break down the door, though he knows she's on the other side. He can't enter her house, nor her body.

At the narrative level, then, *Strait Is the Gate* is about the blindness of love, the inability of the lover to see the beloved clearly. Alissa is *not* as Jerome sees her, just as Marceline is *not* as Michel sees her in *L'Immoraliste*. Jerome projects his weaknesses outwards, onto Alissa. It turns out that Jerome is the uptight person. Alissa is more natural. She trusts her intuition.

In his *Journal*, André Gide wrote in 1937: 'It was only much later, only too late, that I understood what a reliable guide is desire' (J, 609). He wished he had given himself up to his desires more often. It is the same story with many of Gide's characters (and also those of the modern, Greek poet C.P. Cavafy, whose writing and thinking chimes with Gide's at many points).

Like Constantin Cavafy, André Gide mourns his youth and the erotic and sensual promises it held. 'Nathaniel, ah! satisfy your joy while it gladdens your soul', he says in *Fruits of the Earth* (126f). Desire is what makes life exciting. But desire also kills, and, like the Buddhists, Gide would do away with desire if he could ('If only we were not wakened into life again by a fresh onslaught of desire', the narrator complains in *Fruits of the Earth* [129]).

Many of André Gide's characters are in love with images, with projections, with photographs, letters, journals, memories, art – everything except the real thing. They recoil from flesh-and-blood, and take refuge in emotional mediation, in constructs of the imagination. In fantasy, in short.

In the Autumnal melancholy of the short novella *Isabelle* (1911), the narrator falls in love with a photograph. Love is literally blind in *The Pastoral Symphony*. In *The Counterfeiters* nearly all the relationships are failures; they are shallow and ironic, lacking in Stendhalian crystallization. (In *The Counterfeiters*, the narrator say he's more interested in 'decrystallization': 'People are always talking of the sudden crystallization of love. Its slow *decrystallization*, which I never hear talked of, is a psychological phenomenon which interests me far more' [69]).

Most of André Gide's fiction is ironic, self-critical, and bitter at times. His characters love into mirrors, make love with mirrors, just as Gide writes into mirrors. He veers from desire to detachment, from passion to irony. He is reactionary, moving from the indulgence of *The Immoralist* to the renunciation of *Strait Is the Gate*. In an entry of Sunday, November 7, 1909, he says, after finishing *Strait Is the Gate*:

> It will be another ten years before I can again use the words: love, heart, soul, etc... (J, 138)

André Gide is great at using these Platonic words: his natural tendency is to be passionate. But he recoils from romance and tries to keep his distance. He is so restless, ever on the move. The problem with this shape-shifting recourse to irony is that he sometimes feels as if he's never written anything really serious.

ANDRÉ GIDE

These doubts appear in the *Journal*. He aims for a clear, elegant art, in the manner of Stendhal. Gushing sentimentality he hates; yet he wrote in this way in *Fruits of the Earth, Strait Is the Gate, The Notebooks of André Walter* and in many parts of the *Journal*.

The detached, ironic André Gide wrote *The Vatican Cellars* and *The Counterfeiters*, but it's the passionate, volatile Gide of *Fruits of the Earth, Strait Is the Gate* and *André Walter* that is more memorable, and perhaps more valuable. The ironic Gide is the artist of ethics and commentary, the world-weary, Wildean teacher of æsthetics. The emotional, fervent Gide is the self who yearns for God, Christ and love and joy. All of his art up to *The Counterfeiters* he says he wrote for his wife, Madeline:

> My entire work is inclined toward her... I wrote everything to convince her, to win her esteem. It's all but one long plea. (Et, 77)

André Gide is a modern troubadour in this respect, in the tradition of Dante Alighieri loving Beatrice Portinari, or Francesco Petrarch eulogizing Laura de Sade. Alissa is compared to Beatrice (SG, 16), while the main female character in *Les Faux-Monnayeurs* is called Laura.

The Gidean yearning for love begins with *The Notebooks of André Walter* (*Les Cahiers d'André Walter*, 1891). Here André Gide explores his obsession with the Black and the White – the twin poles running between desire and repulsion. He is a Neo-Gnostic here, contrasting soul and flesh. Few books, outside of mysticism, deal so passionately with the idea of 'soul'. Gide may be against mysticism, but this early work is soaked in it. André Walter adores his cousin, Emmanuelle, madly. The whole of *The Notebooks of André Walter* is powered by his yearning: sweet, intense, delicate yearning. Walter wants a soul-union with his Neoplatonic beloved more than anything else. In a self-conscious, mannered and deliberately dense poetic style, Gide enunciates his cult of love:

ANDRÉ GIDE

> Emotions transcend thoughts and yield pure harmony... I hoped that she would receive all my tenderness... "What is the SOUL?" they will ask. The SOUL is our WILL TO LOVE... When you said "My brother" and I answered "little sister", our hearts quivered at the involuntary tenderness of our voices... Only desires matter... Loving, adoring, impassioned caresses – I am obsessed by the act of caressing... Passion subsides; the soul meditates... our souls were transplendent in the mutual reflections of our ecstasy...
> (*André Walter*, pp. 33, 39, 45, 46, 51, 53, 65, 79)

This is the language of passion-filled adolescence, yet André Gide kept writing in this ecstatic mode for his whole life. He keeps his sensualism in check, but it appears now and then in the *Journal*.

In *The Notebooks of André Walter*, as in much of Western poetry since Classical Greek times, God (or the sacred), the beloved, and the poet's *anima,* all mesh together. Sometimes André Walter sends his yearning out towards Emmanuelle, sometimes towards God, sometimes towards his *anima* (or soul), or some projected part of his psyche, and sometimes towards the critic in him, or the sensualist, or the prophet, or the Protestant.

André Gide has many selves, like his characters, like his books (and those multiple selves were developed very early on in his writing career). The book-within-a-book trope is common in Gide's work, as is the soul-within-a-soul. Gide's ultimate subject, though, is himself, or his many selves. It is not the beloved (whether woman or young boy) that fascinates him, nor is it his own experience of love; it is how his love can be transformed into art. Gide is the ultimate artist. He lives for art, for writing. Love is a deep experience for him, yes, but he's just as concerned with how the love-experience can be put into words. What has been learnt? How does love affect the growth of the self? How does love influence art? – these are among the questions Gide asks.

You – you – you... The Noteboooks of André Walter is filled with impassioned cries to the ubiquitous 'you' of Western love poetry (heard in everything from Ancient Greek epigrams to the latest pop songs). This 'you' is God, Christ, love, the beloved, or the poet's soul (or anything you fancy).

Religion and love fuse. In André Gide's philosophy, emotion is prime, above all other considerations. He is subjective and individual, yet he has problems submitting himself to love. He desires it and yet so rarely dives into it.

A typical scene in *The Notebooks of André Walter* is when the lovers are united by music at night: the scene fuses the Gidean concerns of love, art, music (Fréderic Chopin at the piano), sensuality (the storm), memory, desire and detachment:

> We remained silent.
> "Look into the darkness," you finally said, as if alarmed. "Is it not supernatural?"
> Lightning flickered noiselessly on the horizon The air was perfumed with pollen from lime-trees, with the scent of flowering acacias. I tried to take your hand; it was feverous but you rebuffed me.
> We remained silent. (AW, 63)

The Notebooks of André Walter was an obsessive, very introspective work that consumed André Gide (If, 185f). It is freighted with tears, ecstasies, dreams, sleep, prayers, hearts, passions, purity and fever. It is the fruit of sleepless nights in a teenage torpor of infatuation.

André Gide's homoeroticism is as full of tensions as the heterosexual encounters in his books. In *Si le grain ne meurt*, Gide describes a night out with Oscar Wilde: they picked up two Algerian boys; Wilde disappeared into his bedroom with his boy; Gide with the other; after the boy had gone Gide masturbated:

> Long after Mohammed had left me I stayed there in a state of quivering jubilation, and although I had reached the summit of pleasure with him I revived my ecstasy many more times, and back in my

ANDRÉ GIDE

hotel room I relived its echoes until morning. (If, 284-5)

André Gide's autoeroticism manifests itself in his art: as noted above, he writes into mirrors, his characters love into mirrors, and Gide himself has sex with mirrors, with his image reflected in mirrors. Gide's homoeroticism in his fiction is an extension of this autoeroticism (and narcissism is a significant component of his homoeroticism). He is not concerned so much with other people, with the young boys or women, but with himself.

It is typical too that André Gide says he tried to relive the orgasmic encounter in his hotel room afterwards. The *memory* of the act becomes more important than the act itself, and memory for Gide, as for Marcel Proust, serves art. In Gide's output, art triumphs over life, even over the 'wild, burning, sensual and mysterious' part of life which is sexuality (If, 285).

André Gide regarded his love of young boys and masturbation as a vice. He has a Puritan's disgust for the flesh (or is it the Catholicism or Protestantism in him?). He slides from lust to disgust. He tries to keep his distance, to keep everything in perspective. He cannot hide his delight in sex:

In the glorious splendour of evening what radiance bathed my joys! (If, 249)

The homosexual elements in *The Vatican Cellars*, *The Counterfeiters* and *The Immoralist* are reduced in importance and André Gide brings forward his central concerns with art and the growth of the self. Life feeds art, but in Gide's work art is the main means of transcendence-of-self, of sex, and of art itself. (Gide explored the issue of homosexuality in his limited edition *Corydon*, 1925).

CHAPTER NINE

JOY

> Mais émerveillons-nous à présent de ceci: chaque fécondation s'accompagne de volupté. Le fruit s'enveloppe de saveur; et de plaisir toute persévérance à la vie. Pulpe du fruit, preuve sapide de l'amour. (But for the present, let us wonder only at this – that every fecundation is accompanied by pleasure. The fruit clothes itself with flavour; and all urge towards life is enveloped with enjoyment. Pulp of the fruit – the sapid proof of love.)
>
> André Gide, *Fruits of the Earth* (89)

Few artists are as joyful as André Gide. 'Joy' is a better term than ecstasy. Ecstasy is mystical, it speaks of a mystic state of being. Gide, deliberately anti-mystical, speaks of joy, of bliss, of rapture, meaning the simple *joi* of being alive.

The simplest things make his characters happy. A common phrase in the *Journal* is 'radiant weather'. The black and white are reflected in André Gide's art as day and night. His nights are sleepless and difficult, and he dreams and hopes for a 'radiant morning':

ANDRÉ GIDE

the weather was radiant this morning; this is the secret of my happiness. (J, 178)

There are many instances of joy in the *Journal*. It is a joy born from simple sensual delights: the slowburning joy of reading; the radiance of the morning; of travel; and of hope.

Much of André Gide's joy or *jouissance* comes from youth, the dawn, from hope for the future. 'The world of Christ is always fresh with an infinite promise', he mused (J, 271).

Generally, André Gide needs to be relaxed to enjoy himself. His restlessness makes him rush from experience to experience, but his joy requires stillness and contemplation. This is a typical entry in his *Journal* (typical, but not as frequent as complaints of a sleepless night):

> On the Adriatic, May, 1914.
> Voluptuous calm of the flesh, as much at rest as this unruffled sea. Perfect equilibrium of the mind. The free flight of my thoughts is supple, even, bold, and voluptuous, like the flight of these gulls through the dazzling blue. (J, 201)

This is André Gide's ideal state of being: supple, clear, light (water and sky), fresh. Words such as lucid, tranquil and youthful come to mind. It is a state free from doctrine, age, class, gender, politics, religion and mysticism. It is a non-mystical state, this joy: it has no object other than its own beingness. If is not 'for' anything, nor even, often, 'because' of anything. Further, Gide does nothing with his joy. It is necessary, but not necessarily creative. It does not 'go' anywhere, it simply *is*.

Fruits of the Earth is the book of Gidean joy. This suffuses the book, the bliss of rebirth after a period of ascetic renunciation. At times it is a religious realization ('Believe that God and happiness are one' [F, 25]), but more usually a revelation of being alive once more: '*Let every moment renew your vision*' (F, 25).

After the rebirth in Book I of *Fruits of the Earth*, the Gidean self lives in 'an almost perpetual state of passionate wonder' (28). This is the optimum state of being for the artist. After this revelatory experience, the reborn soul demands joy. Joy, *jouissance*, should become the norm. 'Ah! wherever I go, may all things be irradiated with brightness!' (28).

The Gidean self's thirst increases, attaining cosmic dimensions: he demands satisfactions (31), foods of all kinds. Hunger becomes religious. Food becomes poetic. His aim, above all, is the quenching of his divine thirst.

Huge hungers, tremendous thirsts, extravagant expectations – all these are mechanisms of desire, of desire that becomes religious. So André Gide builds up his cult of desire, his gospel of joy. Joy must be spontaneous (33); taken on the wing (37); it must occur in the now, the eternal present (43); regret is jettisoned (82); youth feeds joy (126).

André Gide's joyous gospel in *Fruits of the Earth* pivots around hunger: the deeper the hunger, the more piercing the satisfaction (84). It is full of the desert, of heat, of summer, of travel:

> Tu n'imagines pas, Nathanael, ce que pent devenir enfin cet abreuvement de lumière, et la sensuelle extase que donne cette persistante chaleur... Une branche d'olivier dans le ciel; le ciel au-dessus des collines; un chant de flûte à la porte d'un café... Alger semblait si chaude et pleine de fêtes que j'ai voulu la quitter pour trois jours; mais à Blidah, où je me réfugiais, j'ai trouvé les orangers tout en fleurs...
> (You cannot imagine, Nathaniel, the effect produced by this saturation of light, and the sensual ecstasy that comes from this persistent heat... An olive branch in the sky; the sky above the hills; the song of a flute at a cafe door... Algiers was so hot, so full of rejoicings, that I determined to leave it for two or three days but at Blidah, where I took refuge, I found the orange-trees were in flower... [112])

This is a typical Gidean joy, this evocation of terraces, gardens, balconies, deserts, oases. Joy flows through it all. The image of fruit lies at the heart of the book, fruit that is left on the branch until it is fully ripe. The moment it falls is the moment of

ANDRÉ GIDE

joy. For Gide, this joy is not *like* the ripe fruit, it *is* the fruit. No metaphors for him. Nothing must stand in the way. Joy is also simple: it is, simply, a ripe fruit, or sunlight, or a caress (Rainer Maria Rilke also evoked a poetry of fruit, of ripeness, as an ideal state of beingness).

André Gide remarked: 'the fruit clothes itself with pleasure' (F, 89). All nature is given over to pleasure. No hedonism this, but simple joy. When the farmer 'sings the farm', he 'sings pleasures' (86). The ripe fruit is for the early Gide the image of life, of life in ascension, of life that has struggled free of everything society holds dear (the whole of enculturation):

> And the image of life for me, oh, Nathaniel! is a fruit rich in flavour on lips thirsty with longing. (128)

The joy that fuels *Fruits of the Earth* is not short-lived in André Gide's *œuvre*, though it is tempered later on by irony and detachment. One of the hallmarks of *Later Fruits of the Earth* (1935) was precisely this: joy.

The fruits of *Les nouvelles nourritures* are evoked with a greater sureness in *Later Fruits of the Earth*. André Gide returns to the sensory incantations of the earlier book but makes the message more philosophical. Joy is still very much the goal, and it is already everywhere ('An all-pervading joy suffuses the earth' [143]). Nature teaches joy; joy is in the Earth, the plants, the stars; the initiate's job is to learn this, to realize it, to open up. Here Gide chimes with poets such as Novalis, Percy Bysshe Shelley and D.H. Lawrence – poets from earliest times to the modern Romantics.

André Gide's late joy is perhaps even more intense a joy than before: 'I feel so intense a joy in existing' (F, 145). The fruits of the earth here in this new, joyful world are tenderly caressing other plants (148), The fruit now embodies compassion: it gives itself when it is ripe (156). Altruism and Christianity add weight to

ANDRÉ GIDE

Gide's new joy, but they don't cause it to sink, or affect it much. Now Gide recognizes a 'superhuman effort in the Gospel towards joy' (168). The divine thirsts of the earlier *Fruits of the Earth* have been quenched by nothing humbler than water, for, as Gide notes, 'The true Christian is he whom pure water suffices to intoxicate' (168).

André Gide's later lyricism is not damped at all by forty years of living and writing. Here he is, in his sixties, saying:

> I am amazed at everything on this earth. (175)

Such joy is rare, and is very simple. André Gide now is sure that all the processes of nature tend 'towards pleasure' (189). Fighting against this is no good; you must follow your desires. Life is basically joyous, says Gide, bringing the philosophies of Walt Whitman, Friedrich Nietzsche, Henry David Thoreau, Blaise Pascal and many others to their apotheosis. It is a common feeling in our time, too. Lawrence Durrell believes in a Taoist, Gnostic ecstasy-in-life which just requires the right kind of delicate realization to make it an everyday experience. 'The universe is a big hug with no arms!' Durrell asserts. Joseph Campbell too believes that 'bliss is now', and that it is your duty to make it work. 'Follow your bliss', he encourages in *This business of the gods...*:

> I say to follow your bliss wherever your true inner bliss is, wherever you feel in harmony... The way to find happiness is to keep your mind on those moments when you feel most happy, when you really are happy – not excited, not just thrilled, but deeply happy. This requires a little bit of self-analysis. What is it that makes you happy? Stay with it, no matter what people tell you. This is what I call "following your bliss". (107)

Easy to say, of course. But the basic feeling is right. The problems begin, as Thomas Hardy explored in his novels, when

ANDRÉ GIDE

you try to integrate this bliss-seeking with your relationships with other people – friends, family, lovers, relatives and society.

Before bliss can be achieved, you have to die to yourself. André Gide in the *Later Fruits of the Earth* picks up on one of mysticism's prime objectives: ego transcendence. Gide uses the Christian motif of the fruit needing to die in order to give birth to other fruits:

let it die that you may live. (F, 156)

First, says the narrator, we must die to ourselves, we must strip ourselves of all extraneous material, we must reduce ourselves to essences:

O boy whom I love... Away with your ballast! Let not the weight of the lightest past be a drag upon your freedom. (145)

Get rid of everything – that was Menalcas' urge. Get rid of possessions, of the past, of everything that holds you back. Let it all go. This notion appears later on in *The Immoralist* and *The Counterfeiters*. It was of prime importance to André Gide. Be original, keep moving, be spontaneous, keep fresh.

The self must die – the flower, the fruit, even Winter itself dies, so that new lives can be born. André Gide gives this dying-to-self a Christian slant, but it is the central element in religions such as Buddhism, Hinduism, Taoism and Islam. Indeed, the mystical traditions are even more severe: the less of self, the more room there is for God they say.

Less is more, and the mystic wants as much of God as possible. André Gide, however, wants as much of himself as possible. He wants to birth new selves, to work on them, to nurture them. His aim is self-transcendence – through bliss.

The joy, born in the 1890s, continued to bear fruit. André Gide's ecstasies started off well, however. *The Notebooks of André*

ANDRÉ GIDE

Walter, one of his earliest works, is full of raptures, but they are centred not around simply being alive, but on the poet's love of 'her', the ubiquitous 'you' of literature. The soul, says André 'must be nurtured anew on surges of rapture' (AW, 32). Archetypal, post-Rimbaudian doctrine, this. Souls in ecstasy (79), the stuff of so many Western poets, from Sappho to Rainer Maria Rilke. Here André Gide adds his own voice to those of Giraut de Borneil, Francesco Petrarch, Plotinus, Maurice Scève, Catullus, Alexander Pushkin, Thomas Traherne, and Fakhruddin Iraqi.

André Gide's joyful voice is of its time, though (early-mid 20th century), and can seem dated now. 'Soul' is no new term to Western culture, but the idea of a battle between soul and flesh personified by an angel and a beast taking place within a character's mind, is typically modern, and Symbolist. The world as a single brain or mind is a modern, dramatic concept, present in William Shakespeare's work, but brought to fruition by Samuel Beckett (and in Gaia theory). Gide tries to make an angel, a Rimbaudian/ Rilkean angel. His aim is 'to be angelic' (AW, 78).

Typically patriarchal, André Gide notes that the flesh pulls you down: it has weight and gravity pulls it down, while 'In the angel there is the ever-growing desire to ascend. He must have a *goal* and move towards it', he notes in *The Notebooks of André Walter* (80) It is a spirit-body dichotomy again, one of the central tensions in Western culture. The birth of the self will reconcile the angel and the beast, the poet and the eagle of *Prometheus Misbound*.

But this talk of angels is rhetoric, too super-abundant for André Gide. He is not a poet in the gushing, Baroque sense. His sense of irony weighs down his lyrical flights. *The Black Notebook* records the intensification of André's madness:

> I live in a perpetual state of hyper-excitement... desire torments me... Prepare the night for more ecstatic states...by your silences – stillness, ethereal brightness... I pray, pursue ecstasy... madness is imminent.

ANDRÉ GIDE

(pp. 85, 111, 115, 117, 125)

Arthur Schopenhauer, Immanuel Kant, Charles Darwin *et al* cannot bring the mad soul back to Earth: he starts to utter fevered epithets; worthy of disturbed souls such as St Paul:

> you live because I dream you... it is through me that you live, through me! *I live only through your love.* (AW, 129)

'I dream you' – this ultimate statement of psychic projection is not so very far removed from the famous statement of St Paul:

> For I through the law died unto the law, that I might live unto God. I have been crucified with Christ; yet I live; and yet no longer I, but Christ liveth in me: and that life which I now live in the flesh I live in faith, the faith which is the Song of God. (*Epistle To the Galatians*, 2: 19-20)

Born in the era of Arthur Rimbaud, Paul Verlaine, Comte de Lautréamont and the French poets of intoxication in the late 19th century, Symbolist era, André Gide could not help being influenced by them all. The poet in him wrote the lyrical works which culminate in *The Immoralist, Paludes, André Walter* and *Strait Is the Gate*. But Gide is much more proser than poet, and he knew, as a novelist-in-the-making, that the real challenge was to integrate these passionate night-madnesses into the light of the workaday world. The fiction attempts to do that.

In 1902's *L'Immoraliste* you sense André Gide's sympathy with Michel's exotic, evil-seeking desires. As Michel wakes up, he begins to live the doctrines of *Fruits of the Earth*. He becomes *Fruit*'s Nathaniel, and experiments with the possibilities that life holds. The sleeper awakes, the dreamer cometh, the visionary, after his illness (his old life) slips away, begins to see:

> O Marceline!... Je regarde. Je vois le soleil; je vois l'ombre; je vois la

ligue de l'ombre se déplacer; j'ai si peu à penser, que je l'observe, te suis encore très faible; je respire mal; tout me fatigue, même lire; d'ailleurs que lire? Être, m'occupe assez.
(O Marceline!... love, I see the sun; I see the shadow; I see the line of shadow moving; I have so little to think of that I watch it. I am still very weak; my breathing is very bad; everything, it tires me – even reading; besides, what should I read? Existence is occupation enough. [26])

With the rebirth in *The Immoralist* comes a more sinister belief in the Nietzschean Superman; Charles Darwin's theory of evolution is poeticizied (I, 34). Existence becomes divine (52); joy reveals itself to be his life's target:

And every day my life grew richer and fuller, as I advanced towards a riper, more delicious happiness. (I, 59)

D.H. Lawrence said that everyone must decide for themselves what 'living' actually is. Michel in *The Immoralist* resolves to find out (88). Ménalque arrives to crystallize Michel's life at this point, and reprises the thoughts of *Fruits of the Earth*:

Ah! Michel, toute joie nous attend toujours, mais veut toujours trouver le couche vide, être la seule, et qu'on arrive à elle comme un veuf...
Que chaque instant emporte tout ce qu'il avail s'apporté.
(Ah! Michel! every joy is always awaiting us, but it must always be the only one; it insists on finding the bed empty and demands from us a widower's welcome... Let every moment carry away with it all that it brought. [107])

But as the journey towards self-realization continues, joy is snatched at; it hardens; *ennui* returns; realization finally comes to Michel:

I know now – I have found out at last what gives me my special value. It is a kind of stubborn perserverance in evil. (151)

ANDRÉ GIDE

Joy might be nature's natural state, the state of the flesh, but it is not the soul's typical stance. Humankind fractures reality with its notions of evil, pain, sin, dogma, superiority and exclusiveness.

In the novel *Strait Is the Gate*, joy is fragmented and occurs at a great distance. Jerome cannot connect with Alissa, and Alissa, kept waiting too long, re-aligns her sense of 'living'. In *Strait Is the Gate*, it is Alissa who turns into the angel:

> ...the extraordinary light that shone in her eyes flooded her face with an unearthly, an angelic beauty. (SG, 103)

Alissa becomes an angel, and ascends. She rises without Jerome. He is the one held down by his confused views of the flesh. It is holiness not happiness for Alissa (87), but she is ironic about the whole affair, talking more than a little mockingly of 'some better thing':

> "Can you imagine it, Jerome? – "Some better thing!"" (SG, 104)

No he can't. He is impoverished, creatively. She has more power than him, a deeper sense of what real, deep 'living' is. In those searing letters and the superb journal, Alissa demonstrates how she is transcending herself. She goes way beyond Jerome, beyond his world, dreams, and conceptions. She transcends herself 'beyond love' (114), something he could never do. The idea is anathema to him, the fool so in love with the old ghost of Alissa. She changes; he remains the same. She thinks she holds him back (115), but he can't progress anywhere. He can only follow her, follow her spiritual journey, through her writings. It is a solitary path, she says – 'so narrow that two cannot walk in it abreast' (116). But she is still reaching out for him. Jerome cannot follow.

It is honest of André Gide in *Strait Is the Gate* to admit his character's deficiency, his inability to fly high with women's souls. When Alissa quotes Blaise Pascal – 'Joy, joy, joy, tears of joy' (124) – she is far beyond Jerome. She is high, high, high. Her renunciation (and despair) is complete. She has died to her old self, she has transcended her self; she is an angel, a saint, a martyr. Jerome can only (post-humously) beatify her, like some martyred mediæval saint. Joy overwhelms her:

> Above human joy and beyond all sufferings, yes, I foresee that radiant joy... It is now, at once, that I thirst for happiness... Jerome, I wish I could teach you perfect joy. (125)

In the later works of fiction of André Gide, the concept of joy is squeezed dry by irony. The characters suffer because of this. Everything is restrained. Joys become materialistic (in *The Vatican Cellars*, 81), or part of arid, dialectical debates (in *The Counterfeiters*). There are moments in the latter work when joy is unrestrainedly expressed: Bernard tells how he understands the Fyodor Dostoievsky character who could kill himself 'out of enthusiasm, out of sheer excess of life... just *bursting*' (C, 242). Earlier, of Bernard, the narrator writes:

> He feels as happy as a king. He has nothing left and the whole world is his! (C, 57)

This is the stance of the modern, Existential, social outsider – starting from the bottom, with nothing. As Henry Miller writes on the opening page of his epic trilogy of novels *The Rosy Crucifixion*:

> I was approaching my thirty-third year, age of Christ crucified. A wholly new life lay before me, had I the courage to risk all. Actually there was nothing to risk: I was at the bottom rung of the ladder, a failure in every sense of the word.[7]

To possess nothing but to have the whole world – this is a

very Gidean pose, made even better because of its immensely noble, Christian overtones. It is a good place to start, with nothing, yet to possess the Kingdom of Heaven. It's all inside you; it always has been. As Gide wrote in his *Journal* (227):

> Joy, joy... I know that the secret of your Gospel, Lord, lies altogether in this divine word, Joy.

André Gide by Felix Vallotton, c. 1898

André Gide in Paris in 1894 (above)
Early 1890s (below).

André Gide by Théo van Rysselberghe, 1901

André Gide by Leopold Gottlieb, 1924

André Gide and Marc Allégret, 1920

Gide's wife Madeleine (left).
Gide with his daughter Catherine (below).

The older André Gide
(this page and over)

NOTES

1. D.H. Lawrence: *A Selection From Phoenix*, Penguin, 1971, 188.
2. D.H. Lawrence, op. cit., 185.
3. Robert Graves: *Poems About Love*, "Foreword", Cassell, London, 1987, 6-7
4. Naomi Mitchison: *Travel Light*, Virago, 1985.
5. See Bernard Lonergan: *Method In Theology*, Darton, Longman & Todd, 1971
6. Lawrence Durrell: *Nunquam*, Faber, 1971, 11.
7. Henry Miller: *Sexus*, Calder & Boyars, 1969, 5.

BIBLIOGRAPHY

All books are published in London, England, unless otherwise stated.

ANDRÉ GIDE

F	*Fruits of the Earth*, tr. Dorothy Bussy, Penguin, 1970
I	*The Immoralist*, tr. Dorothy Bussy, Penguin, 1960
C	*The Counterfeiters*, tr. Dorothy Bussy, Penguin, 1966
SG	*Strait Is the Gate*, tr. Dorothy Bussy, Penguin, 1969
VC	*The Vatican Cellars*, tr, Dorothy Bussy, Penguin, 1969
If	*If It Die*, tr. Dorothy Bussy, Penguin, 1977
PS	*The Pastoral Symphony* and *Isabelle*, tr. Dorothy Bussy, Penguin, 1963
AW	*The Notebooks of André Walter*, tr. Wade Baskin, Peter Owen, 1968
Cor	*Corydon*, tr. Richard Howard, G.M.P., 1985
P	*Marshlands* (*Paludes*) and *Prometheus Misbound*, tr. George D. Painter, Secker & Warburg, 1953
Et	*Et nunc manet in te* and *Intimate Journal*, tr. Justin O'Brien, Secker & Warburg, 1952
J	*Journals 1889-1949*, ed. & tr. Justin O'Brien, Penguin, 1967
J2	*Journal 1914-27*, Secker & Warburg, 1948
Am	*Amyntas*, tr. Villiers David, Bodley Head, 1958
So	*So Be It, or The Chips Are Down*, tr. Justin O'Brien, Chatto & Windus, 1960
Pre	*Pretexts; Reflections On Literature and Morality*, ed. Justin

ANDRÉ GIDE

      O'Brien, Secker & Warburg, 1959
OC   *Oeuvres complètes*, Gallimard, Paris, 1932-39

Journals, tr. Justin O'Brien, 4 vols, Seeker & Warburg, 1948-49; Alfred Knopf, New York, 1951
Travels in the Congo, tr. Dorothy Bussy, Penguin, 1986
Selected Letters of André Gide and Dorothy Bussy, ed. Richard Tedeschi, Oxford University Press, 1983
Les nourritures terrestres et les nouvelles nourritures, ed. Claude Martini, Bordas, Paris, 1971
Self-Portraits; The Gide/ Valéry Letters, 1890-1942, ed. Robert Mallet, tr. June Guicharnaud, University of Chicago Press, Chicago, IL, 1966
L'Immoraliste, Mercure de France, Paris 1972/85
Oscar Wilde, William Kimber, 1951
Montaigne: An Essay In Two Parts, tr. Stephen H. Guest & Trevor B. Blewitt, Blackamore Press, 1929
The Logbook of The Coiners, tr. Justin O'Brien, Cassell, 1952
Dostoievsky, Secker & Warburg, 1949
Romans, récits, soties, œuvres lyriques, Bibliothéque de la Pleiade, Paris, 1958
Urien's Voyage, tr. Wade Baskin, Peter Owen, 1964
The Correspondence of André Gide and Edmund Gosse, ed. Linette P. Brugman, Peter Owen, 1960
Oedipus and Theseus, tr. John Russell, Secker & Warburg, 1950
The Return of the Prodigal Preceded By Five Other Treatises With Saul, tr. Dorothy Bussy, Secker & Warburg, 1953
The School for Wives; Robert and Genevieve, tr. Dorothy Bussy, Cassell, 1953

ANDRÉ GIDE

OTHER WORKS

Miriam Allot, ed. *Novelists on the Novel*, Routledge, London, 1963
Christopher Bettison. *Gide: A Study*, Heinemann, 1977
Georges Bataille. *Literature and Evil*, tr. Alistair Hamilton, Calder & Boyars, 1973
M. Haskell Block & Herman Salinger, eds. *The Creative Vision: Modern European Writers On Their Art*, Grove Press, New York, 1960
Paul Bowles. *Their Heads Are Green*, Abacus, 1990
Germaine Bree. *Gide*, Rutgers University Press, New Jersey, 1963
—. *Camus and Sartre: Crisis and Commitment*, Calder & Boyars, 1974
Geoffrey Brereton. *An Introduction To the French Poets*, Methuen, 1960
—. *A Short History of French Literature*, Penguin, 1976
Joseph Campbell. *The Power of Myth*, with Bill Moyers, Doubleday, New York, 1988
—. *This business of the gods...*, Windrose Films Ltd, Ontario, Canada, 1989
Albert Camus. *The Outsider,* tr. Stuart Gilbert, Penguin, 1961
—. *The Happy Death*, tr. Richard Howard, Penguin, 1973
O. Chadwick. *Rimbaud*, Athlone Press, 1977
J.C. Cooper. *An Illustrated Dictionary of Symbols,* Thames & Hudson, 1978
Thomas Cordle. *André Gide*, Macmillan, 1976
Malcolm Cowley, ed. *Writers At Work: The Paris Review Interviews*, Secker & Warburg, 1958
John Cruickshank. *French Literature and Its Background,* 5 & 6, Oxford University Press 1969/ 70
Yvonne Davet. *Autour Les Nourritures Terrestres*, Gallimard, Paris, 1948
J.C. Davis. *Gide: L'Immoraliste and La Porte Etroit,* Arnold, 1968
Jean Delay. *The Youth of André Gide,* tr. June Guicharhaud, University of Chicago Press, 1963
Laura Doan, ed. *The Lesbian Postmodern*, Columbia University Press, New York, 1994
Paul Éluard. *Uninterrupted Poetry: Selected Writings*, tr. Alexander, New Directions, New York, 1975
John Ferguson. *An Illustrated Encyclopædia of Mysticism*, Thames & Hudson, 1976
Gustave Flaubert. *Madame Bovary*, tr. Gerard Hopkins, Oxford University Press, Oxford, 1981

ANDRÉ GIDE

Wallace Fowlie. *André Gide*, Macmillan, New York, 1965
—. *A Guide To Contemporary French Literature*, 1976
G.S. Fraser. *The Modern Writer and His World*, Penguin, 1964
Ralph Freedman. *The Lyrical Novel*, Oxford University Press, 1963
E. Grosz. *Sexual Subversions*, Allen & Unwin, London, 1989
—. *Volatile Bodies*, Indiana University Press, Bloomington, IN, 1994
—. "Refiguring Lesbian Desire", in L. Doan, 1994
—. *Space, Time and Perversion*, Routledge, London, 1995
Albert J. Guerard. *André Gide*, Harvard University Press, Cambridge, MA, 1951
Howard Hugo, ed. *The Portable Romantic Reader*, Viking Press, New York 1957
Anthony Hartley, ed. *The Penguin Book of French Verse*, vols. 3 and 4, Penguin 1958/66
J-K Huysmans. *À Rebours*, tr. R. Baldick, Penguin, 1959
Jean Hytier. *André Gide*, tr. Richard Howard, Constable, 1963
G.W. Ireland. *Gide*, Oliver & Boyd 1963
J. Kristeva. *Powers of Horror: An Essay on Abjection*, tr. Leon S. Roudiez, Columbia University Press, New York, 1982
—. *The Kristeva Reader*, ed. Toril Moi, Blackwell, 1986
—. *Tales of Love*, tr. Leon S. Roudiez, Columbia University Press, New York, 1987
W. La Barre. *The Ghost Dance*, Allen & Unwin, London, 1972
Jacques Lacan and the École freudienne. *Feminine Sexuality*, Macmillan, 1982
David Little John, ed. *Gide: A Collection of Critical Essays*, Prentice-Hall, New Jersey, 1970
Klaus Mann. *André Gide and the Crisis of Modern Thought*, Dennis Dobson, 1958
Elaine Marks & Isabelle de Courtivron, eds. *New French Feminisms: an Anthology*, Harvester Wheatsheaf, Hemel Hempstead, Herts., 1981
James C. McLaren. *The Theatre of André Gide*, Johns Hopkins Press, Baltimore, 1953
Patricia Merivale. *Pan the Goat-God: His Myth in Modern Times*, Harvard University Press, MA, 1969
Jeffrey Meyers. *Homosexuality and Literature 1890-1930*, Athlone Press, 1977
Michel de Montaigne. *Montaigne's Essays*, 3 vols, tr. John Florio, Everyman/Dent, 1965

ANDRÉ GIDE

Harry T. Moore. *Twentieth-Century French Literature*, Heinemann, 1969
Justin O'Brien. *Portrait of André Gide: A Critical Biography*, Secker & Warburg, 1953
George D. Painter. *André Gide: A Critical Biography*, Weidenfeld & Nicolson, 1968
Walter Pater. *The Renaissance*, Oxford University Press, 1986
Donald Prater. *A Ringing Glass: The Life: Rainer Maria Rilke*, Clarendon Press, Oxford, 1986
Mario Praz. *The Romantic Agony*, tr. Angus Davidson, Oxford University Press, 1933
Joyce H. Reid. *The Concise Oxford Dictionary of French Literature*, Oxford University Press, 1976
Jeremy Mark Robinson. *Blinded By Her Light; The Love Poetry of Robert Graves*, Crescent Moon, 1991
—. *Thomas Hardy and John Cowper Powys: Wessex Revisited*, Crescent Moon, 1991/ 2008
Arthur Rimbaud. *Complete Works*, tr. Wallace Fowlie, University of Chicago Press, Chicago, IL, 1966
—. *Morning of Ecstasy: Selected Poems*, Crescent Moon, 2008
Vinio Rossi. *André Gide*, Columbia University Press, New York, 1968
Bertrand Russell. *A History of Western Philosophy*, Allen & Unwin, 1971
Arthur Schopenhauer. *Essays and Aphorisms*, Penguin, 1970
M.A. Screech. *Montaigne and Melancholy*, Duckworth, 1983
Enid Starkie. *André Gide*, Bowes & Bowes, 1953
Stendhal. *De l'Amour*, tr. G. Sale, Penguin, 1975
D.L. Thomas. *André Gide: The Ethics of the Artist*, Secker & Warburg 1950
Michael Tilby. *Gide: Les Faux-Monnayers*, Grant and Cutler, 1981
Martin Turnell. *The Novel In France*, Hamilton, 1950
—. *The Art of French Fiction*, Hamilton, 1959
Paul Valéry. *Occasions, The Collected Works of Paul Valéry*, vol. II, tr. Roger Shattuck & Fredrick Brown, Routledge, 1971
—. *Moi*, tr. Marthiel & Jackson Matthews, Routledge, 1971
—. *An Anthology*, ed. J. Lawler, Routledge, 1977
David H. Walker. *André Gide*, Macmillan, 1990
—. *Les Nourritures Terrestres and La Symphonie Pastorale*, Grant and Cutler, 1990
Helen Watson-Williams. *André Gide and the Greek Myth*, Oxford University Press, 1967
W.D. Wilson. *André Gide: 'La Symphonie Pastorale'*, Macmillan, 1971

ANDRÉ GIDE

Ludwig Wittgenstein. *Tractatus Logico-Philosophicus*, tr. Pears and McGuiness, Routledge 1961

WEBSITES

andregide.org
gidiana.net

In the Dim Void

Samuel Beckett's Late Trilogy: *Company, Ill Seen, Ill Said* and *Worstward Ho*

by Gregory Johns

This book discusses the luminous beauty and dense, rigorous poetry of Samuel Beckett's late works, *Company, Ill Seen, Ill Said* and *Worstward Ho*. Gregory Johns looks back over Beckett's long writing career, charting the development from the *Molloy-Malone Dies-Unnamable* trilogy through the 'fizzles' of the 1960s to the elegiac lyricism of the *Company* series. Johns compares the trilogy with late plays such as *Ghosts, Footfalls* and *Rockaby*.

Bibliography, notes. Illustrated. 120pp
ISBN 9781861712974 Pbk and ISBN 9781861712608 Hbk
9781861713407 E-book

Beauties, Beasts, and Enchantment

CLASSIC FRENCH FAIRY TALES

Translated and with an Introduction
by Jack Zipes

A collection of 36 classic French fairy tales translated by renowned writer Jack Zipes. *Cinderella*, *Beauty and the Beast*, *Sleeping Beauty* and *Little Red Riding Hood* are among the classic fairy tales in this amazing book.
Includes illustrations from fairy tale collections.
Jack Zipes has written and published widely on fairy tales.

'Terrific... a succulent array of 17th and 18th century 'salon' fairy tales'
- *The New York Times Book Review*

'These tales are adventurous, thrilling in a way fairy tales are meant to be... The translation from the French is modern, happily free of archaic and hyperbolic language... a fine and sophisticated collection' - *New York Tribune*

'Enjoyable to read... a unique collection of French regional folklore' - *Library Journal*

'Charming stories accompanied by attractive pen-and-ink drawings' - *Chattanooga Times*

Introduction and illustrations   612pp.   ISBN 9781861712510 Pbk   ISBN 9781861713193 Hbk

ANDREI TARKOVSKY

JEREMY MARK ROBINSON

POCKET GUIDE

Andrei Tarkovsky is one of the great filmmakers of recent times.

This book covers every aspect of Tarkovsky's artistic career, and all of his output, concentrating on his seven feature films: *Ivan's Childhood*, *Andrei Roublyov*, *Solaris*, *Mirror*, *Stalker*, *Nostalghia* and *The Sacrifice*, made between 1962 and 1986.

Part One of this study focusses on the key elements and themes of Andrei Tarkovsky's art: spirituality; childhood; the film image; poetics; painting and the history of art; the family; eroticism; symbolism; as well as technical areas, such as script, camera, sound, music, editing, budget and production.

Part Two explores Tarkovsky's films in detail, with scene-by-scene analyses (in some cases, shot-by-shot). Tarkovsky emerges as a brilliant, difficult, complex and poetic artist.

Fully illustrated. This new edition has been revised and updated.
ISBN 9781861713957 Pbk   9781861713834 Hbk

ARTS, PAINTING, SCULPTURE

web: www.crmoon.com • e-mail: cresmopub@yahoo.co.uk

The Art of Andy Goldsworthy
Andy Goldsworthy: Touching Nature
Andy Goldsworthy in Close-Up
Andy Goldsworthy: Pocket Guide
Andy Goldsworthy In America
Land Art: A Complete Guide
The Art of Richard Long
Richard Long: Pocket Guide
Land Art In Great Britain
Land Art in Close-Up
Land Art In the U.S.A.
Land Art: Pocket Guide
Installation Art in Close-Up
Minimal Art and Artists In the 1960s and After
Colourfield Painting
Land Art DVD, TV documentary
Andy Goldsworthy DVD, TV documentary
The Erotic Object: Sexuality in Sculpture From Prehistory to the Present Day
Sex in Art: Pornography and Pleasure in Painting and Sculpture
Postwar Art
Sacred Gardens: The Garden in Myth, Religion and Art
Glorification: Religious Abstraction in Renaissance and 20th Century Art
Early Netherlandish Painting
Jasper Johns
Brice MardenLeonardo da Vinci
Piero della Francesca
Giovanni Bellini
Fra Angelico: Art and Religion in the Renaissance
Mark Rothko: The Art of Transcendence
Frank Stella: American Abstract Artist
Alison Wilding: The Embrace of Sculpture
Vincent van Gogh: Visionary Landscapes
Eric Gill: Nuptials of God
Constantin Brancusi: Sculpting the Essence of Things
Max Beckmann
Gustave Moreau
Caravaggio
Egon Schiele: Sex and Death In Purple Stockings
Delizioso Fotografico Fervore: Works In Process 1
Sacro Cuore: Works In Process 2
The Light Eternal: J.M.W. Turner
The Madonna Glorified: Karen Arthurs

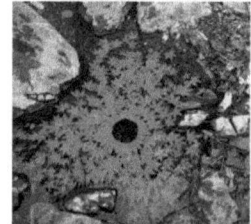

LITERATURE

J.R.R. Tolkien: The Books, The Films, The Whole Cultural Phenomenon
J.R.R. Tolkien: Pocket Guide
Beauties, Beasts and Enchantment: Classic French Fairy Tales
Tolkien's Heroic Quest
Brothers Grimm: German Popular Stories
Sexing Hardy: Thomas Hardy and Feminism
Thomas Hardy's *Tess of the d'Urbervilles*
Thomas Hardy's *Jude the Obscure*
Thomas Hardy: The Tragic Novels
Love and Tragedy: Thomas Hardy
The Poetry of Landscape in Hardy
Wessex Revisited: Thomas Hardy and John Cowper Powys
Wolfgang Iser: Essays and Interviews
Petrarch, Dante and the Troubadours
Maurice Sendak and the Art of Children's Book Illustration
Andrea Dworkin
Cixous, Irigaray, Kristeva: The *Jouissance* of French Feminism
Julia Kristeva: Art, Love, Melancholy, Philosophy, Semiotics and Psychoanalysis
Hélene Cixous I Love You: The *Jouissance* of Writing
Luce Irigaray: Lips, Kissing, and the Politics of Sexual Difference
Peter Redgrove: Here Comes the Flood
Peter Redgrove: Sex-Magic-Poetry-Cornwall
Lawrence Durrell: Between Love and Death, East and West
Love, Culture & Poetry: Lawrence Durrell
Cavafy: Anatomy of a Soul
German Romantic Poetry: Goethe, Novalis, Heine, Hölderlin
Novalis: *Hymns To the Night*
Feminism and Shakespeare
Shakespeare: *The Sonnets*
Shakespeare: Love, Poetry & Magic
The Passion of D.H. Lawrence
D.H. Lawrence: Symbolic Landscapes
D.H. Lawrence: Infinite Sensual Violence
The Ecstasies of John Cowper Powys
Sensualism and Mythology: The Wessex Novels of John Cowper Powys
Amorous Life: John Cowper Powys (H.W. Fawkner)
Postmodern Powys: New Essays on John Cowper Powys (Joe Boulter)
Rethinking Powys: Critical Essays on John Cowper Powys
Paul Bowles & Bernardo Bertolucci
Rainer Maria Rilke
Joseph Conrad: *Heart of Darkness*
In the Dim Void: Samuel Beckett
Samuel Beckett Goes into the Silence
André Gide: Fiction and Fervour
Jackie Collins and the Blockbuster Novel
Blinded By Her Light: The Love-Poetry of Robert Graves

POETRY

Ursula Le Guin: *Walking In Cornwall*
Peter Redgrove: Here Comes The Flood
Peter Redgrove: Sex-Magic-Poetry-Cornwall
Dante: Selections From the *Vita Nuova*
Petrarch, Dante and the Troubadours
William Shakespeare: *The Sonnets*
William Shakespeare: Complete Poems
Blinded By Her Light: The Love-Poetry of Robert Graves
Emily Dickinson: Selected Poems
Emily Brontë: Poems
Thomas Hardy: Selected Poems
Percy Bysshe Shelley: Poems
John Keats: Selected Poems
John Keats: Poems of 1820
D.H. Lawrence: Selected Poems
Edmund Spenser: Poems
Edmund Spenser: *Amoretti*
John Donne: Poems
Henry Vaughan: Poems
Sir Thomas Wyatt: Poems
Robert Herrick: Selected Poems
Rilke: Space, Essence and Angels in the Poetry of Rainer Maria Rilke
Rainer Maria Rilke: Selected Poems
Friedrich Hölderlin: Selected Poems
Arseny Tarkovsky: Selected Poems
Paul Verlaine: Selected Poems
Novalis: *Hymns To the Night*
Arthur Rimbaud: Selected Poems
Arthur Rimbaud: *A Season in Hell*
Arthur Rimbaud and the Magic of Poetry
D.J. Enright: By-Blows
Jeremy Reed: *Brigitte's Blue Heart*
Jeremy Reed: *Claudia Schiffer's Red Shoes*
Gorgeous Little Orpheus
Radiance: New Poems
Crescent Moon Book of Nature Poetry
Crescent Moon Book of Love Poetry
Crescent Moon Book of Mystical Poetry
Crescent Moon Book of Elizabethan Love Poetry
Crescent Moon Book of Metaphysical Poetry
Crescent Moon Book of Romantic Poetry
Pagan America: New American Poetry

MEDIA, CINEMA, FEMINISM and CULTURAL STUDIES

J.R.R. Tolkien: The Books, The Films, The Whole Cultural Phenomenon
J.R.R. Tolkien: Pocket Guide
The *Lord of the Rings* Movies: Pocket Guide
The Ghost Dance: The Origins of Religion
The Cinema of Hayao Miyazaki
Hayao Miyazaki: *Princess Mononoke*: Pocket Movie Guide
Hayao Miyazaki: *Spirited Away*: Pocket Movie Guide
The Peyote Cult
HomeGround: The Kate Bush Anthology
Tim Burton : Hallowe'en For Hollywood
Ken Russell
Cixous, Irigaray, Kristeva: The *Jouissance* of French Feminism
Julia Kristeva: Art, Love, Melancholy, Philosophy, Semiotics and Psychoanalysis
Luce Irigaray: Lips, Kissing, and the Politics of Sexual Difference
Hélene Cixous I Love You: The *Jouissance* of Writing
Andrea Dworkin
'Cosmo Woman': The World of Women's Magazines
Women in Pop Music
Discovering the Goddess (Geoffrey Ashe)
The Poetry of Cinema
The Sacred Cinema of Andrei Tarkovsky
Andrei Tarkovsky: Pocket Guide
Andrei Tarkovsky: *Mirror*: Pocket Movie Guide
Walerian Borowczyk: Cinema of Erotic Dreams
Jean-Luc Godard: The Passion of Cinema
Jean-Luc Godard: Pocket Guide
John Hughes and Eighties Cinema
Ferris Buller's Day Off: Pocket Movie Guide
The Cinema of Richard Linklater
Liv Tyler: Star In Ascendance
Blade Runner and the Films of Philip K. Dick
Paul Bowles and Bernardo Bertolucci
Media Hell: Radio, TV and the Press
Detonation Britain: Nuclear War in the UK
Feminism and Shakespeare
Wild Zones: Pornography, Art and Feminism
Sex in Art: Pornography and Pleasure in Painting and Sculpture
Sexing Hardy: Thomas Hardy and Feminism

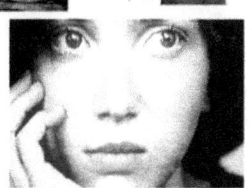

The Light Eternal is a model monograph, an exemplary job. The subject matter of the book is beautifully organised and dead on beam. (Lawrence Durrell)
It is amazing for me to see my work treated with such passion and respect. (Andrea Dworkin)
Sex-Magic-Poetry-Cornwall is a very rich essay... It is like a brightly-lighted box. (Peter Redgrove)

CRESCENT MOON PUBLISHING P.O. Box 1312, Maidstone, Kent, ME14 5XU, Great Britain
0044-1622-729593 cresmopub@yahoo.co.uk www.crmoon.com

www.ingramcontent.com/pod-product-compliance
Lightning Source LLC
Chambersburg PA
CBHW070158100426
42743CB00013B/2955